For Todd,
my best friend
and husband

CONTENTS

ONE · RAINING CATS AND DOGS

JANUARY 1926: WASHINGTON, DC

It seemed like a typical winter day when Maris Boggs, a small woman wrapped in a big fur coat, walked briskly to the bus stop near the corner of Twelfth and F Streets in Washington, DC, just under a mile from the White House. But Maris was about to discover it was anything but.

Although it was a little after noon, the sun was hidden behind dark clouds, making it feel more like dusk. The fierce wind was unrelenting, saturated with a bitter icy rain. The bus held the promise of warmth and coziness, but it had not yet arrived.

Maris noticed a candy shop with a covered doorway, and she took shelter there, hoping to stay warm and dry from the razor-sharp wind and sleet. While she was waiting anxiously for the bus, she suddenly felt something brush up against her ankle. Startled, Maris peered down through her glasses and saw a shivering puppy with bedraggled white fur, brown ears, and two little brown patches on his back.

He looked up at her pleadingly with his brown-green eyes and tried to wag his tail, but he was too cold. Maris reached down and petted him. The puppy leaned in closer to her, snuggling into her soft fur coat and enjoying the warmth from the touch of her small hand.

"Why, you poor thing!" Maris said. "You must be nearly dead."

Looking around, Maris wondered if the puppy's owner might be in the candy shop. She opened the door, and the puppy dashed inside with Maris following closely behind him. They were immediately enveloped by the warmth of the shop, and by the sweet, heavenly scents of sugar, chocolate, vanilla, licorice, and mint.

She asked the storekeeper and customers if

they knew who the puppy belonged to, but no one knew anything. Realizing the puppy was either lost or abandoned, Maris picked him up and held him in the crux of her arm. She had a dilemma.

Maris couldn't keep the puppy, but she also knew if she left him, he would die from the cold. The solution proved to be simple. She would just have to take the puppy with her to work and keep him until she found his owner or a new home.

Luckily, she was the boss, so no one in the office was likely to complain about the puppy this one time. Maris, who had recently celebrated her thirty-seventh birthday, was the cofounder and director of the Bureau of Commercial Economics, a nonprofit organization founded in 1913.

Maris's mission in life was to spread goodwill throughout the world. She was a globe-trotting world traveler who hobnobbed with political leaders and diplomats. Maris believed that if people learned about other cultures, they would have a better understanding of one another. As a result, Maris felt people would get along better and create world peace.

Her organization promoted goodwill by showing educational movies about different cultures and countries to millions of people all over the world, free of charge. This was an innovative idea, and in the beginning, some people were unsupportive. At the time, showing movies in movie theaters had only been around for about twenty years, and back then, going to the movies was looked down on as a lowly form of entertainment.

But Maris didn't listen to the naysayers. She spread goodwill with eight "traveling motion picture theaters," which were specially equipped trucks that transported a movie projector, a phonograph, a generator, a movie screen, and an assortment of silent black-and-white films. These trucks traveled all over the United States and were loaded onto ships and sent to continents as far away as Asia, Africa, and South America. And if the trucks couldn't travel over roads to the more remote villages, she would have the equipment loaded on camels, llamas, or dogsleds — whatever it took to get the job done.

Now Maris had another mission — to find the puppy a good home. So when the bus finally arrived, Maris carried the puppy on board.

The rule for bringing a dog on the bus was

strict, even for a quick ten-minute bus ride. The puppy was only allowed on the bus if he sat on Maris's lap. This kept big hulking dogs like Saint Bernards and Great Danes off the bus. Maris's puppy looked like a fox terrier, and he was so small he wouldn't bother anyone. Or so she thought.

The bus was crowded, and Maris found an empty seat by squeezing in between a plump man in an expensive suit who was busy reading a magazine, and a woman who was clutching a large shallow basket on her lap.

As the bus clamored down the busy street, dropping people off and letting others on, the puppy started to squirm. As tired and hungry as he was, the woman's basket had sparked his curiosity. He needed to know what was inside.

The tiny puppy stretched his scraggy body out across Maris's lap and unabashedly stuck his wet nose into the basket. He discovered it was full of vegetables. Satisfied, he wagged his stubby tail enthusiastically, knocking into the plump man's magazine.

The woman holding the basket quickly placed a newspaper over the vegetables, not wanting dog germs contaminating them. The man folded up his magazine in a huff, his concentration broken.

Maris was embarrassed. But before she had a chance to explain his plight to her fellow passengers, the bus came to a halt. It was her stop. She held the puppy protectively in her arms, walked by the scowling bus driver, and exited the bus.

When she arrived at her office with the tired and hungry puppy, she asked her secretary what they should feed him. The secretary rushed to the store and bought some hamburger meat. But when they tried to feed it to him, the puppy didn't take a bite. He soon fell asleep under Maris's desk.

Maris worked diligently for the rest of the afternoon. When five o'clock rolled around and it was time to go home, Maris was presented with another problem. No dogs were allowed in her apartment building. But Maris wasn't going to let this foil her plan.

When she arrived at the grand Beaux-Arts style building she called home in the neighborhood of Mount Pleasant, she avoided the front entrance. Stealthily, she went around to the back of the massive beige-colored brick building. Holding the puppy in one arm, Maris climbed up the fire escape. When she reached her apartment's window on the top floor, she carefully climbed through it with the puppy.

Once safely inside, the puppy took a good look around his new home. It was posh and spacious with large French doors that opened onto a stone balcony. Maris introduced him to the maid, who took a good look at him.

The puppy was very thin and malnourished, and Maris expressed worry that he hadn't eaten. Since he refused to eat the hamburger meat, which was something she figured all dogs would gobble up, she didn't know what to feed him. When her maid suggested dog biscuits, the puppy's brown ears twitched and his face perked up. He seemed to understand.

Dog biscuits were promptly purchased at the store, and when the puppy was given some, he ate with so much gusto he tried to eat the cardboard box, too. Finally satisfied and with a full stomach, he curled up on the plush carpet and quickly fell into a deep, deep sleep.

Over the next several weeks, Maris realized he was a puppy like no other. His intelligence and natural curiosity were already evident. Whenever anything interested him, he tilted his head to the side and gave it a good sniff. He was also developing an independent streak. He steadfastly refused to respond to snapping fingers or the command "Here, boy!"

As much as Maris loved the puppy, she knew she couldn't keep him. It wasn't fair to keep him hidden inside her apartment all day, every day. She wanted him to have an exciting life, one full of adventures befitting such an intelligent and strong-minded dog. But she had no idea who would want a puppy.

Then, one day while she was reading the newspaper, she came across an article on Richard Evelyn Byrd. At thirty-seven years old, the handsome and intrepid aviator was making headlines with his plan to be the first person ever to fly over the North Pole — a daring feat that many considered crazy.

In 1926, aviation was an extremely dangerous profession. People were still trying to figure out the best way to build airplanes, and they were considered somewhat experimental. It was a given that pilots would more than likely get hurt, if not killed, in a crash.

On top of that, flying in the Arctic was extremely hazardous. The Arctic winds could blast a plane off course, navigating in the icy and snowy Arctic fog was nearly impossible, and the subzero temperatures might cause a plane's engine and parts to fail, causing it to crash.

"The easiest way a man can make a monkey of himself is to take up Arctic exploration work by airplane," Byrd once said.

Despite this, Byrd had recently wowed the world when he became the first person to fly an airplane in the Arctic over Greenland. But that wasn't the first time the world took notice of his adventurous spirit.

In 1902, when Byrd was a skinny, freckle-nosed fourteen-year-old living in Winchester, Virginia, a family friend invited him for a visit to their new home in the Philippines. Byrd wanted to go in the worst way. He thought this was the perfect opportunity for him to take a trip around the world — all by himself.

When he told his mother his plans, she immediately said no. But Byrd was determined. After some convincing, his mother reluctantly changed her mind.

"Richard was born an adventurer and explorer, absolutely without fear," his mother said.

He packed his new suitcase with a pair of extra underwear, two neckties, a pocketknife, and a ball of string. His mother insisted on traveling with him from Winchester to Washington, DC, where they said good-bye. Then he boarded a train that took him to San Francisco.

"That day my face was full of poison oak and I could hardly see because my eyes were so swollen," Byrd said. "My mother was not given to weeping, but she wept that day. I felt more than a little blue myself."

In San Francisco, he boarded the transport ship *Sumner*, where Mrs. Wendell, a friend of his uncle's, traveled with him. After they made it to their first port in Japan, a major typhoon struck, tossing the ship at sea and making everyone sick. But Byrd was having the time of his life.

"I thought that was a wonderful storm," Byrd said. "I didn't know enough to be afraid."

After Byrd arrived in the Philippines, he traveled alone throughout Asia, Europe, and Africa. On his return trip home, the ship got lost, but that didn't upset Byrd.

"I was tickled to death," he said. It also ignited Byrd's interest in navigation.

"I don't suppose I had ever thought much about navigation before," Byrd said. "I knew the compass was necessary . . . but I did not know that time was part of the calculation for determining position. Navigation became at once a mysterious and important function."

When Byrd finally arrived back in New York more than a year later, he was greeted and interviewed by a dozen newspaper reporters.

Soon after Byrd returned from his trip around the world, he enrolled at Shenandoah Valley Military Academy. The above photo is Byrd at fifteen years old.

Everyone wanted to know about his trip around the world.

It was at this time Byrd knew, without a doubt, that he wanted to be an Arctic explorer. And even though he hated cold weather, he hoped to be the first person to set foot on the North Pole.

He read everything he could get his hands on about the Arctic and the explorers. Although Byrd was not a stellar student in school, there were two subjects he excelled in — mathematics and navigation. Byrd knew these two subjects were essential if he wanted to find his way to the North Pole.

But, when he was twenty years old and a student at the U.S. Naval Academy, Byrd's dream was dashed when polar explorer Robert Peary proclaimed that he was the first person to reach the North Pole.

"The day that Peary discovered the North Pole was the darkest day of my life," said Byrd.

This wasn't the only setback to derail his dream.

At the Naval Academy, Byrd was a fierce and reckless athlete. Although he was average in height and very lean, Byrd was really strong and powerful. He loved the rough-and-tumble sport of football, where he went all out as the quarterback. During a showdown with archrival Princeton, Byrd was tackled in a pileup. The crowd in the stands cheered enthusiastically. Byrd had scored a touchdown.

But Byrd was lying on the field, unable to stand up. His foot had been crushed and was broken in three places. His teammates gathered around him and carried him off the field. His football season was over.

Nevertheless, Byrd was just as enthusiastic in gymnastics. His favorite event was the flying rings. During his final year at the Naval Academy, Byrd was determined to help his team win big. So he came up with a daredevil routine that he called "the dislocating."

Byrd explained that the dislocating routine required swinging "completely head over heels without changing grip, with arms at full length — unbending, forcing my shoulders through a quick jerk that made it look as if they were put out of joint."

He was certain it was going to dazzle the

judges. But they never had a chance to see it. While practicing the dislocating routine in front of a crowd, Byrd swung around and missed catching the rings. He could hear the crowd gasp in horror while they watched him fall thirteen feet to the mat below.

"The crash when I struck echoed from the steel girders far above me, and there was a loud noise of something snapping," said Byrd.

The loud snapping noise was his foot — the same foot that he broke while playing football.

The routine landed Byrd in the hospital with a dislocated ankle and broken foot. The outside anklebone was broken in half and clicked every time he tried to walk, causing extreme pain. The doctors operated on his foot and wired it back together.

A studious Byrd hitting the books.

Byrd spent the next five months trying to recover, and from his hospital bed, he studied feverishly, barely squeaking by in his classes. Although he still managed to finish the school year and graduate from the Naval Academy on time, his injured foot would nearly ruin his career.

Byrd began his career in the navy on board the battleship USS *Kentucky* and was soon transferred to the USS *Wyoming*. His foot continued to cause excruciating pain, affecting his entire leg, especially when he had to stand for hours at a time while on watch duty.

"Certain kinds of deck duty left me aching all over from the pain that began in the old mangled ankle," said Byrd.

But the final blow came when Byrd fell down an open gangway and broke his foot for a third time. The doctors nailed the broken bones back together, but Byrd's foot was never the same. From that day on, he would walk with a slight limp. Soon after, he retired from the navy.

"Career ended," Byrd wrote. "Trained for a seafaring profession; temperamentally disinclined. A fizzle."

However, a few months later, in the winter of 1917, the United States entered World War I, and

Byrd rejoined the navy. He dreaded being stuck behind a desk doing paperwork, but he had a new plan.

"For several years, I had known my one chance of escape from a life of inaction was to learn to fly," Byrd said.

He tried to talk the navy into assigning him to the aviation program, but the doctor who examined his foot and leg said no. Byrd couldn't fly.

"Give me a chance," Byrd pleaded. "I want to fly. Give me a month of it; and, if I don't improve to suit you, I'll do anything you say."

The doctor reluctantly agreed, giving Byrd a month's trial.

Byrd was sent to Naval Air Station Pensacola in Florida to learn how to fly, which he did with his usual all-out gusto. He crashed his plane twice — once in a head-on collision. Luckily, no one died.

"He used to go up with anyone who even said he could fly. He risked his life more times than any other beginner I ever saw," said Lawrence Shea, a pilot who taught Byrd.

When Byrd earned his wings, making him a full-fledged navy pilot, his goal was to be a pioneer in the budding field of aviation and to make himself invaluable to the field. At the time, air navigation was a big problem. Pilots navigated using a compass and a map while looking out the window for landmarks. No one dared to fly out of sight of land or over the vast ocean on long flights.

Byrd solved this problem. He developed the "bubble sextant," an air navigation instrument that indicates the pilot's position. Instead of having to look for land, the navigator looks through the sextant and locates his position based on the

Byrd takes a reading with the bubble sextant to determine his position. This is the same sextant he would use on his flight over the North Pole.

altitudes of the sun or stars. Byrd also invented the "drift indicator," an instrument that told a navigator how far off course the winds had blown his airplane.

Byrd's inventions revolutionized air navigation, opening the doors for the possibility of flying airplanes over the ocean and the snow-covered Arctic. And Byrd would be using these inventions on his flight to the North Pole.

When Maris finished reading the newspaper article and seeing the photo of Byrd, she realized that she had met him before. She knew in that instant Byrd would give her puppy an exciting life. She immediately called him and offered him the puppy. But Byrd didn't want him.

"Don't you like dogs?" Maris asked.

"Certainly I like them," Byrd said with a slight southern drawl. "I have had many dogs, and several of them were the most loyal friends I ever had. But they died. And because I had become so deeply attached to them, their deaths always affected me brutally. You can understand that, I think. That is why I don't want another one."

Maris wouldn't give up, "I know you will like

him. In fact, if you persist in this dangerous business of flying to the Poles, I daresay he will probably outlive you."

But Byrd wasn't convinced.

"I don't think it would be a good idea to take a dog, and especially a puppy, to the polar regions," Byrd said. "It's very cold, you know, and he might freeze to death."

Maris was dogged in her determination. She wouldn't take no for an answer. "If a man can stand it, a dog can stand it," she said.

Byrd didn't know what to say to that, and he reluctantly agreed to take the puppy.

"You had better rush him to New York," Byrd said. "Because we are planning to leave in a few days. Our ship is nearly loaded now."

Maris wasted no time. She found a large wicker basket, put the puppy inside along with two wool sweaters, a dog collar, two leashes, a bar of sweet-smelling soap, a brush, and a comb. She wrote out the address on a piece of paper and attached it to the lid of the basket. It read, "Lieutenant Commander Richard E. Byrd, the North Pole."

Soon the puppy would be on top of the world.

ON TOP OF THE WORLD

TWO

APRIL 5, 1926: BERTH 10, CLINTON AVE., BROOKLYN NAVY YARD, NEW YORK

Below the rusty and tar-covered decks of the steamship SS *Chantier*, in the galley where all of the meals were cooked, the puppy whined. A metal chain was attached to his dog collar. He pulled the chain with all his might, trying to break free from it, but it was no use. He couldn't escape.

After a few more attempts, the puppy realized it was futile, and he changed tactics. He sat down and waited, his brown ears twitching while he listened anxiously for approaching footsteps.

Once he heard them, he planned on barking like a rabid, mad dog. Until then, he would just have to sit tight, which is exactly what Byrd and the crew wanted.

Everyone was too busy to be bothered with the puppy, and his ferocious barking didn't help make him seem friendly or approachable. Truth be told, many on the ship thought the puppy was a pest. Even so, they did take the time to name him. Some called him Frosty. Others called him Dynamite. But the name Igloo stuck.

The chain attached to his collar was there for his own good. No one wanted Igloo to run away

The SS *Chantier* in New York Harbor.

or get underfoot. Everyone was busy, trying to get the ship loaded and ready for its departure as quickly as possible.

The lanky, good-natured carpenter Charles "Chips" Gould was hammering furiously, trying to insulate the ship's quarters with sugarcane fiber. The quarters would have to keep the crew warm when they arrived in Spitsbergen, Norway, their starting point for Byrd's flight to the North Pole. Byrd chose Spitsbergen because its distance to the North Pole was only 720 miles. That was close enough to allow Byrd to fly to the North Pole and back without having to risk landing on the deadly ice to refuel and take off again.

Byrd was in a hurry to start the journey. It would take about a month to reach Spitsbergen from New York. And it was crucial that Byrd reach the North Pole in May when it would still be too cold for thick fog to form. Fog would seriously jeopardize his mission. There also needed to be snow covering the rocky terrain so the plane had a better chance of landing safely when it returned from the North Pole. But Byrd was also in a hurry to get to Spitsbergen before Norwegian polar explorer Roald Amundsen arrived.

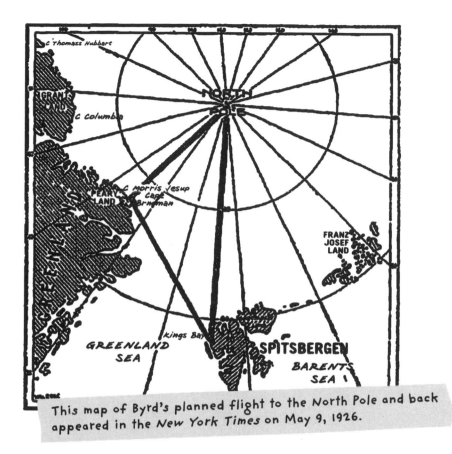

This map of Byrd's planned flight to the North Pole and back appeared in the *New York Times* on May 9, 1926.

Hailed as the "King of All Living Explorers," Amundsen was the first person to set foot in places where other men died trying. He was the first to find the elusive Northwest Passage and the first in the race to reach the South Pole. Now he had set his sights on being the first to fly over the North Pole, just like Byrd.

This wasn't Amundsen's first try. The year before, he and American polar explorer Lincoln

Ellsworth and four others tried to fly two planes over the North Pole. They were nearly killed when they lost their way in the fog and one of their planes had mechanical problems, forcing them to crash-land in the floating ice–filled water. Their planes quickly froze over, and walls of ice closed in all around them.

Using the only tools on hand — axes, picks, knives, and an ice anchor — it took them a month to cut one of the planes out of the ice and build an ice bridge across a chasm. By hacking, sawing, and stomping down on the ice over and over again, they were able to build an airstrip of smooth ice. With their emergency rations nearly gone, the starved and exhausted men narrowly escaped with their lives as they miraculously flew one of the planes back to safety.

This time Amundsen wasn't going to try to fly an airplane over the North Pole. Instead, he was going to fly a dirigible. A dirigible, or blimp, is a lightweight aircraft that can travel long distances without having to land and refuel.

"There isn't a safe place to land a heavy plane with skis between Cape Mitre and the Pole," Amundsen said. "If you come down in open water, and there is a lot of it, you haven't a chance. And if you try to land on the deceptive ice, it means a crash. In any event, motor failure means wreckage of the plane, ninety-nine times out of one hundred. And it's a long and dangerous walk home, over open leads and rotten ice, for two men without dogs and with limited rations."

Despite Amundsen's vast experience and legendary reputation as the "last Viking," Byrd boldly disagreed with him.

"Our great aim is to show what the airplane can do," Byrd said. "Secondly, it is to find new land. Thirdly, it is to try to reach the Pole by air."

Byrd's choice of airplane was the most important decision in planning the flight. After careful consideration, he decided to fly a trimotor monoplane named the *Josephine Ford*, which was built by a Dutch aircraft company called Fokker. Byrd knew a plane wasn't always dependable, but he figured a three-engine plane was the answer to a successful flight over the North Pole. If two engines failed, the plane could still fly with one engine and avoid an emergency landing.

He also chose the calm, cool, and gutsy pilot-mechanic Floyd Bennett to accompany him.

They'd become fast friends the year before when they flew 2,500 miles over the Greenland ice cap together, where Byrd was the navigator and Bennett was the pilot.

"He showed that he was a good pilot . . . fearless and true — one in a million," Byrd said of Bennett.

Once during a flight on the Greenland expedition, Byrd noticed the oil gauge quickly

Byrd standing in front of an airplane he flew in the Arctic with Floyd Bennett on the MacMillan Greenland expedition.

rising, indicating the oil tank was ready to explode. There was nowhere to land the plane without crashing. It was a do-or-die situation.

Without hesitation, Bennett climbed out onto the plane's wing. With the Arctic wind blowing and the plane bouncing up and down, Bennett loosened the oil cap, relieving the pressure and saving their lives. The frostbitten Bennett then climbed back into the plane, and they successfully completed their flight.

Byrd and Bennett were a good team, and despite Amundsen's warning, they were determined to fly over the North Pole in an airplane.

"True, we realized the hazardous nature of the flight," Byrd said. "Experienced polar travelers told us we were fools. The fog which lies over the Arctic Ocean would add to the already great risks; and, if we came a cropper [crashed], it would take us, they said, at least two years to walk back to land, if we ever made land at all. Nevertheless, these were risks we were prepared to take."

Byrd was careful in all of his planning, which was evident in the cargo being loaded onto the ship. There were stacks and stacks of wooden crates, trunks, and steel barrels filled with supplies piled high throughout the ship. The food supplies alone contained four hundred pounds of emergency rations of pemmican (a mixture of lean, dried meat, cereal, suet, lard, currants, raisins, and spices that is heated over a stove with water turning it into a mush), 4,500 pounds of whole carcasses of beef, and another eight tons of other food, including eggs, sausage, bacon, oatmeal, dried milk, butter, sugar, cream cheese, and pea soup. There were enough provisions to feed the fifty men who had eagerly volunteered to be the crew aboard the ship for three months.

The two planes Byrd planned to use on the expedition were the trickiest of all the cargo to load onto the *Chantier*. Byrd watched the men load the Fokker trimotor monoplane and the yellow-and-orange Curtiss single-engine Oriole. The Oriole would be used only as a scouting plane. If the Fokker met with disaster, the scouting plane was not able to travel long distances on rescue missions.

It took a nail-biting six hours to load the sixty-three-foot red wing from the body of the *Josephine Ford* safely on board. The clanking sound of chains and the rumble of the gears shifting were loud as a crane hoisted the wing up into the air. It hovered over the opened hatch, where the men stood on ladders as they carefully eased it into the hold below deck. But it was too big to fit, and it became stuck.

Everyone was quiet for a brief moment, as if time stood still. The men grabbed some axes and began chopping away the bulkhead that was in the way. Little by little the wing was lowered until it finally fit and was safely secured without a scratch.

While Byrd and his crew got the ship in shape, Igloo wallowed in his misery down in the galley. But it wasn't all doom and gloom for him. There was one particularly bright spot, the gregarious carrot-topped cook with the wire-rimmed glasses, George "Cook" Tennant.

Cook Tennant tried to cheer up Igloo with some treats. It worked for a bit. He was an excellent cook with plenty of experience feeding hungry mouths. He had sold hot dogs at the World's Fair in Saint Louis, baked pies for oil riggers in California, and cooked on fishing and sealing ships in Alaska.

But on this day, even Cook Tennant was too

busy for Igloo. It was midafternoon, too early for dinner, when Igloo heard footsteps approaching the galley. The footsteps came closer and closer, and Igloo began barking loudly. When Igloo looked up, he saw a stout, dark-haired man looking down at him. Igloo wagged his tail, happy to see him.

It was Igloo's other new friend, Tom Mulroy. He was the chief engineer of the *Chantier*, and Mulroy was not put off by Igloo's wild barking. He was impressed that a puppy's bark could sound "like a lion's roar."

Mulroy unhooked Igloo's chain, allowing Igloo to trot along beside him as they left the galley. Mulroy often took Igloo for a "walk," deep into the bowels of the ship to the hot and steamy engine room where Igloo could inspect the pumps, pipes, coils, valves, generators, furnace, and boiler. The ship's after hold contained the nine hundred tons of coal that would be used to feed the furnace and power the ship for 15,000 miles.

But today Igloo was in for a surprise. Instead of going down to the engine room, Mulroy and Igloo went to the upper deck of the ship.

Igloo walked among the crates, hoses, and equipment on the deck. When Igloo looked up, he saw a flag with an American eagle on it waving in the wind on the ship's masthead. When he looked to the bow of the ship, Igloo could see Byrd standing tall, wearing his navy-blue dress uniform and waving his hat to 2,000 people lined up on the pier. The crowd was cheering and bidding them farewell.

While the tugboats pushed the freshly painted black-and-red *Chantier* out of the harbor, the crowd shouted as the other tugs and steamers in the harbor sounded their whistles and sirens. Swept up in the excitement of the moment, Igloo rushed to the side of the deck and barked, joining in with the crowd to cheer.

For the first several days, the sea was rough. Waves rolled the ship back and forth as rain pummeled down. Everyone on board was seasick — except Igloo.

Unleashed, Igloo was having a ball running as fast as he could up and down the stairs between the decks, trying to time it just right as the ship rolled back and forth. When Igloo wanted a change of pace, he went up onto the main deck, and he ran as fast as he could until he reached the end of the ship, where he let out a bark of delight. Then he'd start all over again.

But sometimes his timing was off, and the ship would roll to one side while Igloo was in midsprint, sending him flying across the slippery deck. With his legs flailing, he plunged headfirst toward the mouth of the ocean, only to be caught by the railing of the ship. On these hair-raising occasions, when Igloo cheated death, he would forgo the bark and slink back to his starting point. Then he would do it all over again.

While Igloo was busy making mad dashes around the decks, the square-jawed captain of the *Chantier*, Michael Brennan, was struggling to steer the ship. It turned out that the weight from the coal in the after hold was too heavy, causing the rear of the *Chantier* to sink down lower into the ocean. All hands were called on deck. Byrd and his queasy, seasick crew spent days breaking their backs moving the coal from the after hold to the midship coal bunkers. But it didn't dampen their enthusiasm.

"No one considers seasickness any cause to give up," said Byrd.

Even though the crew members were busy,

several of them caught a glimpse of Igloo zipping by and nearly being swept overboard. They told Byrd about it, and he was concerned. From that moment on, Byrd took Igloo under his wing.

Igloo was delighted by this new arrangement. When Igloo first met Byrd, he had immediately liked him, and had enjoyed the quick, short walks Byrd had taken him on around the deck. During these walks, Igloo noticed that among all of the men on the ship, Byrd was the top dog. Whenever Byrd gave an order, his crew complied.

Igloo immediately moved in to Byrd's stateroom, bringing along his favorite new toy, a stuffed goat that he enjoyed pouncing on and wrestling with. Despite the upgrade of his sleeping accommodations, one stormy night Igloo couldn't catch a wink of sleep.

The wind howled ruthlessly and giant waves pounded the ship, violently rocking it back and forth. A table crashed down, and Igloo found himself being tossed among books, papers, and shoes. When there was a sudden moment of calm, Igloo jumped up onto the foot of Byrd's bed. And in that instance, Igloo knew he belonged by Byrd's side.

Soon after, Igloo refused to eat in the galley, no matter how hungry he was — unless Cook Tennant pressed him. Then he might have a nibble, but no more. Instead, he gallantly followed Byrd into the dining room and took his place by Byrd's chair. After everyone had helped themselves, Byrd would fix a plate for Igloo and serve it to him. Igloo ate with relish.

While at sea, Byrd and Bennett spent most of their time planning their flight, not wanting to miss any details. Their main concern was a crash. Sometimes, Igloo sat in on these discussions, preferring to sit on Byrd's lap.

"We are flying in dangerous country," Byrd wrote in his diary. "The three hundred miles to Greenland is the most hazardous region in the world to fly over. If we should have a forced landing there we would be swept in to [sic] the Atlantic before we could cover fifty miles and the ice would melt under us."

If the plane crashed between Peary Land, a mountainous peninsula in northern Greenland, and the North Pole, Byrd and Bennett would have to walk back, dragging a sled with 240 pounds of pemmican. The pemmican would last for sixty days. They would also carry a rifle so they could hunt polar bears and seals for food, and they would bring a tent and an inflatable twelve-pound "donut" boat that was made of hot-air balloon cloth and could carry six hundred pounds of passengers and cargo.

Along with the six-pound first-aid kit, which contained splints and bandages, the Yale-educated Dr. Daniel O'Brien, who was the expedition's medical officer, also gave Byrd and Bennett instructions on how to perform surgery in case one of them was severely injured in a crash.

Byrd and Bennett were also concerned about the weight of the plane. If the cargo was too heavy, the plane would burn more gasoline, and they might not get to the North Pole and back.

"The weight has to be kept down to a minimum and yet there are so many things we should have to add to our safety," said Byrd.

Byrd spent time carefully weighing all of the equipment and cargo, but he wouldn't know exactly how much they could take until they tested out the plane in Spitsbergen.

Sometimes while Byrd was busy planning,

Igloo skipped out and explored the ship. One of his favorite stops on board was the radio room. Whenever he found the door to the radio room open, Igloo would sneak in, lie down, and pretend to nap. With his eyes half open, he would watch the sandy-haired Malcolm Hanson busily working out the bugs in the new cutting-edge shortwave radio station.

The radio was a crucial piece of technology for Byrd. His plane would be equipped with a receiver and transmitter, allowing him to receive weather reports and send back progress reports while in flight.

The radio headset Hanson wore fascinated Igloo. One time, it fell to floor, and Igloo went over to investigate. Tilting his head to one side, Igloo listened to the noise coming from it. When Hanson tried to pick it up, Igloo barked three times, letting Hanson know that under no circumstances was he to touch the headset until Igloo was finished studying it. Hanson, who was known to be as smart as a whip, complied.

After twenty-four days at sea, with the help of an ice skipper, whose specialty was navigating ships through the dangerous iceberg-filled waters, the *Chantier* reached King's Bay in Spitsbergen, Norway at 4 p.m. on April 29. Byrd was relieved that they had arrived right on time, but the relief was short lived. He quickly realized that despite his hasty departure, he was too late.

Amundsen was already there. And he was almost ready to start his flight to the North Pole. He was just waiting for his dirigible to arrive from Italy.

The two men were in a race to be the first to fly over the North Pole. And, despite all of his careful planning, Byrd had no idea about the kind of trouble that was in store for him.

APRIL 29, 1926: SPITSBERGEN, NORWAY, THE ARCTIC CIRCLE

From the moment the *Chantier*'s rusty anchor dropped into the icy King's Bay, trouble was brewing. Igloo stood on the upper deck where he had a bird's-eye view of the ship and harbor.

He was wearing one of his new wool sweaters at the insistence of his friend Tom Mulroy. At first, Igloo wasn't sure if he liked wearing it. The sweater felt bulky and cumbersome, and it somehow seemed wrong for any self-respecting dog to have to wear it. But it did fend off the bitter Arctic air that chilled his bones. And all of the men were wrapped up in warm winter clothes, too. So Igloo grudgingly accepted it.

There was a flurry of nonstop action on deck, and Igloo didn't want to miss out. The trouble for Byrd began when he radioed Amundsen. Byrd politely asked Amundsen to help make arrangements for the *Chantier* to be moored to the only dock in the harbor. Byrd also offered to help Amundsen in return, if he should need it.

The dock was critical to Byrd's plan. It was the only place where he could unload his airplanes. If he didn't have access to the dock, then he would fail before even having a chance to try to fly over the North Pole. In the months before embarking on his long journey, Byrd had cabled ahead to the local manager of the dock and asked if he would be able to secure the *Chantier* there. Byrd was told that it wouldn't be a problem. But today it was a different story.

"Greatly disappointed today to hear from Amundsen by radio that we could not go alongside dock," Byrd wrote in his diary.

The reason was that a dark gray Norwegian gunboat, the *Heimdahl*, was already moored at the dock and resupplying its store of coal.

The crew from the *Heimdahl* was preparing to assist Amundsen when his dirigible arrived and to help him with any emergency he might experience while in King's Bay. Trying to find a solution, Byrd asked Captain Tank-Nielsen of the *Heimdahl* directly if the *Chantier* would be able to moor there for a few hours, just so Byrd could unload his planes.

The captain said no. The *Heimdahl* had nearly sunk a few days earlier when drifting ice rammed into the ship. The captain feared if his ship left the safety of the dock, an unexpected shift in the wind would cause more ice to ram into the *Heimdahl*. The captain wasn't budging. And Byrd was told it would be days before he would be allowed to use the dock.

Byrd realized it was no use arguing, but he wasn't about to give up. He had an idea that the rest of his crew thought was crazy. But Byrd was willing to risk it all.

"We may be licked," Byrd wrote in his diary, "but don't want to be licked waiting around and doing nothing . . . All opposed to my decision. They were wise probably."

It was the time of year in the Arctic when the

sun never sets — when the Earth is tilted on its axis, so the Arctic is always facing the sun. And Byrd could easily read the newspaper by sunlight at 3:30 in the morning. Since the days felt like they had no beginning or end, it would allow Byrd's crew to work through the night without taking a break to sleep. There wasn't a moment to spare if Byrd's new plan was going to work.

With a hammer in his hand, the hardworking ship's carpenter, Chips Gould, and the crew got busy. They tied together four lifeboats and hammered wooden planks across them. They worked all night long. The wind felt raw and snow fell steadily, accumulating chilly, thin layers on their backs.

By early morning the makeshift raft was built. The snow was falling harder now and the ice floes were getting thicker in the water. Igloo watched the crane reach down into the hold of the ship and lift a large crate up into the air. The snowflakes whirled around as the crate was lowered onto the deck. When the crate was broken open, Igloo trotted over to investigate. Curious, he tilted his head to the side and sniffed around the body of the Fokker airplane.

The body of the *Josephine Ford* airplane being lowered onto the makeshift raft.

Everyone was tense while the airplane was lowered carefully onto the raft and securely tied. Next, Igloo watched the crane lift the wing of the plane into the air. It hung heavily. As it was positioned to be lowered onto the body of the plane, a sudden gust of wind kicked in. The force of the wind slammed the raft into the side of the iron ship.

The men struggled to secure the wing to the deck with ropes and move the raft to the stern of the ship. Suddenly, the ferocious wind pushed a gigantic iceberg toward the ship. The iceberg was about to crash into the ship's rudder. The crew quickly grabbed some dynamite and threw it at the iceberg, blowing it up into small pieces and saving their ship.

For the next twelve hours, the storm was merciless, and waves and ice thrashed against the ship. Despite the fierce cold, the crew stood guard, fending off runaway ice floes and protecting the raft and wing from blowing away or sinking. When Byrd finally turned in to sleep that night, he got up every hour to check the ice. By morning, the wind finally died down and the ice was floating calmly in the water. Byrd gave the go-ahead to lower the wing onto the raft.

"If anything slips," Byrd said while the wing was hanging dangerously in the air, "the expedition comes to an end right now."

Everyone breathed a sigh of relief when the wing was secured to the fuselage. But now the most difficult part of Byrd's plan began. The *Chantier* was anchored about three hundred feet from the shore, and a strong gust of wind or wave could easily topple the raft, sinking them all. To make matters worse, the sharp and jagged ice was so thick and packed together so tightly that it looked like a person could walk right over it all the way to the shore without getting his feet wet. But looks were deceiving.

Luckily, Byrd received some much-needed help from Norwegian Captain Astrup Holm, whose cargo ship the *Hobby* was being chartered by Amundsen and was nearby. Captain Holm circled the *Chantier* and cut the ice away from it. He then got into a small boat with Byrd's ice pilot, Norwegian Isak Isaksen, who had thirty years of experience in the Arctic Ocean. Together, using boat hooks, ice picks, and sheer brute force, they chopped the ice and shoved it out of the way, carving out an opening and exposing the deep black water.

Byrd gave the order to begin rowing the raft through the watery path despite being very worried.

"It was anxiety for my shipmates that made that trip a most anxious one for me," Byrd said. "I felt entirely responsible for their safety."

But Igloo was on the raft with Byrd, giving his full support to the endeavor. It was slow going. Many of the men had never rowed a boat before, and one was using his oar backward. The crew struggled to keep the ice from pounding into their fragile raft, using their oars and long poles to push it out of the way. But the poles and oars were of no use when they were more than one hundred yards from the *Chantier* and two massive icebergs towered over them. They carefully wedged their raft between the icebergs, knowing that they "could have crushed us like nuts in a nutcracker," Byrd said.

Nevertheless, they made it.

And Byrd wrote in his diary that it was a lot of fun. "Got cheers from Norwegians, which we returned," he wrote. "Norwegians didn't think we would make it."

For the next thirty-six hours, Byrd and his crew worked nonstop. Igloo stuck close by, keeping an eye on their progress.

"If it was a very big undertaking for my men to get the plane ashore," Byrd said. "It surely was a muscle-tearing job for them to get the plane and equipment up to the top of the long incline through the deep snow."

The plane had to be assembled and a runway had to be made by digging and smoothing out the snow with shovels. This proved to be the hardest job of all. Since there wasn't any level ground, they would have to try to take off going downhill.

Cook Tennant set up a tent near the plane and brewed strong hot coffee. The coffee helped keep the crew warm. At times the temperature dipped to fifteen degrees below zero, and everybody's feet

Unloading the *Josephine Ford* airplane from the makeshift raft.

were cold, especially Igloo's. His wool sweater, now stained with oil, wasn't always warm enough against the harsh weather, and he shivered.

On these occasions his friend Tom Mulroy would lend him his jacket and place Igloo on a crate. Even so, there were times that Igloo couldn't stop shivering. Although he was stoic and uncomplaining, Igloo was sent back to the anchored ship where he warmed his paws by the heat of the stove in Cook Tennant's galley. But as soon as he could feel his paws again, he was eager to get back by Byrd's side, where he belonged.

While Igloo was busy fending off frostbite and trying to convince a crew member to take him back to the action, the first attempt at a trial flight was made. May 3 was a day of reckoning for Byrd.

"Bennett and I were not half so worried about breaking our necks on the polar ice as we were about smashing our plane on the takeoff," Byrd said.

If the plane crashed, it could be the end of the expedition.

Byrd and Bennett got into the cockpit of the Fokker. The plane's motors roared to life and it jetted down the icy runway. Suddenly, there was an ominous silence, and the plane skidded uncontrollably right into a snowdrift.

Hearts sank in disappointment. The plane was damaged. A ski was shattered and the landing gear was mangled. It was a disaster.

"The forward right ski split and fitting torn loose around the fuselage. Very discouraging but we will not get discouraged," Byrd wrote in his diary.

The plane needed new skis, but there wasn't any hardwood to be found. Even so, this wasn't going to stop Byrd and his crew. They would have to make do with what they did have. The carpenter, Chips Gould, and Tom Mulroy took the oars from a lifeboat and worked tirelessly through the next two nights making new skis for the plane.

Byrd also received some unexpected help. Despite Amundsen's orders that his crew stay away from Byrd, one crew member, a twenty-five-year-old Norwegian named Bernt Balchen came over anyway and introduced himself. The blond, blue-eyed Balchen was a middleweight boxing champion, a champion skier, and held an engineering degree. More important, he had been a pilot in the Royal Norwegian Navy Air Service, and he also had lots of experience flying in cold weather. When he offered to help Byrd, he didn't know it was the beginning of bigger things to come.

"We've used a mixture of paraffin and resin on the runners and found it very effective," Balchen told Byrd. "You see, about this time of the year, when the snow begins to melt, the friction is greater. If you use this mixture, I don't think you'll have so much trouble."

But even with the new skis, Byrd and Bennett were still having trouble getting the plane to lift off.

"We were having difficulties . . . in getting off the snow with the lightest possible load. What would happen when we tried our total load of about 10,000 pounds?" Byrd said.

It wasn't until the third try that Byrd's plane finally lifted off. He and Bennett flew the plane for two hours in a test run. They were happily surprised there was low gas consumption. This meant there was a good chance they could make a nonstop, round-trip flight to the North Pole and back. They knew firsthand that taking off and landing midroute was too risky.

Still, Byrd couldn't begin his flight to the North Pole until he received a decent weather report from the meteorologist on the trip, good-natured Bill Haines. Haines, who everyone called "Cyclone," was always calm, slow, and methodical — unless there was an emergency. Then he moved like a cyclone. His skill as a meteorologist was critical to Byrd's success. If the weather report was wrong, it could spell disaster for Byrd and Bennett.

Byrd was still waiting for good weather on the morning of May 7. It was shortly after 10 a.m., and Igloo was standing next to him when they heard the hum of an engine. Igloo looked into the sky. It wasn't Byrd's airplane making the noise. It was Amundsen's dirigible looming overhead. It circled around and lowered itself to the ground by its hangar on the snow-covered hill, right behind Byrd's runway and two hundred yards from his airplane.

The race to the North Pole was back on, and whatever lead Byrd had was now gone. It was full speed ahead.

On May 8, Cyclone Haines informed Byrd that the weather was finally good for flying. Igloo, who had been keeping an eye on Cook Tennant in the field kitchen, heard the commotion by the plane and scurried over to find out what was happening.

Byrd was carefully checking the navigational instruments while the food and fuel were being loaded onto the plane. The motors — which were covered with canvas hoods that had small openings at the bottoms where a small gasoline stove was placed to heat them — were warmed up and ready to roll.

Since there was no heater in the Fokker airplane, and the temperature in the cabin of the plane could easily drop to fifty degrees below zero while flying, Byrd and Bennett were wearing polar-bear-fur pants and hooded reindeer-fur parkas with mittens and boots to ward off frostbite. They would also wear goggles during the flight to prevent snow blindness from the glare of the white snow and ever-present sun.

Igloo stood among the crowd of men from both Byrd and Amundsen's crew. Everyone had gathered to bid Byrd and Bennett farewell. Igloo watched them board the Fokker airplane, and he waited anxiously for the plane to take off.

Byrd (center), Floyd Bennett (right), and George Noville (left) stand in front of the *Josephine Ford* before Byrd and Bennett take flight.

The plane zoomed down the runway, bouncing awkwardly over the frozen snowy bumps. As it reached the end of the runway, it was clear that it was too heavy to lift off. Igloo watched in horror as the plane crashed into a snowdrift, nearly flipping over onto its side.

Igloo sprinted, his frozen paws kicking up the snow like dust as he charged to the plane. He was frantic to see if Byrd and Bennett were okay. Igloo felt utter relief when he saw Byrd climb out of the plane.

"So you're here, fella," Byrd said to him. "Well, you have just seen something that neither you nor I will forget in a long time."

Sick with disappointment, Byrd plowed through the deep snow to check the landing gear. His sinking heart soared when he saw that the skis were still in perfect condition.

"I knew that if the landing apparatus would stand the strain," Byrd said, "we would eventually take off for the Pole with enough fuel to get there."

But first they had to lighten the load on the plane.

"There is a lot of stuff in that plane that must be thrown out," Byrd said.

The first to go was five hundred pounds of gasoline. And upon closer inspection of the cabin, Byrd and Bennett found about two hundred pounds of stuff that was secretly hidden by the crew. The stuff consisted of trinkets, such as flags, pictures, and hats that the crew wanted to make the trip over the North Pole so they would have souvenirs. All the extra stuff was taken off the plane — except for a ukulele that was too well hidden.

Byrd decided that if the weather was still good, they would try again at midnight when the night air was colder, making the snow harder and easier for the plane to take off. He held Igloo in the crux of his arm and boarded a lifeboat, which he rowed back to the *Chantier* to get some rest before trying again. Neither he nor Bennett had slept in thirty-six hours. Bennett was so exhausted he slept in a sleeping bag in the snow next to the plane, while the crew worked around him, getting the plane ready.

At half past midnight, the sun was shining brightly. Tom Mulroy woke Bennett up.

"All ready," Mulroy told him.

A crew member was sent to the *Chantier,* and he alerted Byrd and Igloo that the plane was ready. Byrd and Igloo took a motorboat through the icy waters back to the plane. Byrd knew this was his last chance.

"We were on the ragged edge of failure, and we couldn't spare an ounce of weight," Byrd said. "As it was, we had cracked up three times in the snow already. One more smash and it would all be off."

The runway had been carefully iced in front of the plane's skis so they could get a quick and smooth start. The engines were warmed up. Byrd and Bennett had one last meeting before heading down the runway. They agreed to go full speed ahead: "Get off or crash."

With the motors thundering and the propellers whipping up a cloud of snow, Tom Mulroy took his ax and sliced the rope that tied the plane to a stake in the icy runway. Holding his hands on the throttles, Bennett went full speed ahead.

The plane shot down the runway, Igloo chasing after it, all the way down the hill. The plane accelerated, and as it reached the end of the runway, it soared into the air. Igloo looked up and watched Byrd take flight. Then he strutted with satisfaction.

As the Fokker plane flew over the ice-filled bay, it climbed higher and higher, passing over Cape Mitre and reaching an altitude of 2,000 feet. At that moment, Byrd realized he was really on his way to the North Pole. He thought it seemed too good to be true.

On the horizon Byrd could see the ice glint —

the shimmering light where the ice and sky met under the bright sun.

"There lay our goal," said Byrd. "Through that shining curtain we must pass to whatever lay beyond."

But there were no landmarks on the vast white ice to guide them — there was only the sun. They were relying on Byrd's navigation skills and tools — the sextant, the drift indicator, and a sun compass to determine their position. Briefly, the thought haunted him.

"Would it be sufficient?" Byrd thought. "Would charts I had and knowledge I had gained of variations be enough to pilot us from land to that indeterminable point — the Pole — and back again?"

The thought quickly escaped his mind once he got to work.

Every three minutes Byrd took readings from the drift indicator and sun compass and made calculations with absolute precision.

"I was jumping from one instrument to another," he said.

There wasn't much room to work. The cramped cabin was filled with one-hundred-gallon tanks, radio equipment, loose cans of gasoline, a sled, their food stash, a tent, a rifle, ammunition, smoke bombs, and other emergency landing supplies. This left a narrow aisle for him to walk through, but his bulky fur suit made it a tight squeeze.

Behind one of these tanks was a trapdoor in the floor, which Byrd opened so he could take readings from the drift indicator. Behind the trap door was a shelf where Byrd kept his maps and a sun compass that he used for taking readings through a window.

There was another trapdoor in the roof of the plane. Byrd stood on a box so he could stick his head out the trapdoor. With his nose and cheeks burning from frostbite, he took readings from a sun compass that was attached to the plane's fuselage.

Directly under the roof's trapdoor there was a large compass. Since the needle on a compass is a magnet, the compass was placed under the trapdoor so it wouldn't be affected by the metal on the airplane, which could cause the compass to go haywire. This is known as *local magnetism*. Byrd also had to take into account the compass's fluctuations in this part of the world. The force of the magnetism isn't as strong, causing it to fluctuate. And once the plane passed the magnetic North Pole, which was 1,200 miles to the south of the geographic North Pole (the northernmost point on Earth), the needle of the compass no longer pointed to north — it pointed south.

"We knew our greatest danger was getting off course and that we must fly a straight course to reach the Pole," Byrd said.

Every half hour or when the gasoline got low, Byrd took over the controls and piloted the plane so Bennett could take a break or pump fuel into the tanks from inside the plane. Byrd kept ahold of the sun compass while flying to take readings and adjust their course.

They were about an hour from the North Pole when Byrd discovered another danger. He looked out the cabin window and saw oil fly by him. A rivet had popped off, and the oil tank had sprung a leak. If the motor ran out of oil, it would die, leaving only two engines. The roar of the engines was too loud for Byrd to talk to Bennett, so he wrote him a note.

At first, Bennett thought they should land the plane. He wrote back, "That motor will stop."

They both knew it was too dangerous. If they

tried to land or take off, they risked crashing. And they were so close to reaching the North Pole.

"There was no way we could get at the tank," Byrd said. "And after an exchange of notes, we decided we could keep on to the Pole, come what may."

They went back to work. At 9:02 a.m., on May 9, 1926, Byrd made a note in his diary, which read, "We should be at the Pole now. Make a circle and I will take a picture. Then I want the sun."

For the next few minutes they circled the Pole and enjoyed the idea that they had "circled the world" in no time flat. The North Pole was a stretch of vast frozen snowy white ice.

"It did not look different from other miles of ice over which we had just passed," Byrd said.

To mark the occasion, Byrd and Bennett shook hands. Bennett smiled happily at Byrd, and Byrd felt relief for the first time.

"I realized we had accomplished our purpose," Byrd said.

They decided to head back. The oil was still leaking badly, but the worst was yet to come.

A strong gust of wind suddenly jerked the plane, tipping it to its side. The sextant fell off the shelf, crashing to the floor and breaking. Byrd's most important instrument was useless. The only way they could make it back now was by using a map, clock, and compass — a process known as *dead reckoning.*

But to find their way back to Spitsbergen by dead reckoning, Byrd needed a landmark to determine his current position. The sun was his only guidepost. Using his latest measurements, he quickly calculated the sun's new position. He only had once chance to get it right or he and Bennett risked getting lost for good.

Byrd waited anxiously for the exact time to tell Bennett to fly the plane directly toward the sun. When the time was right, Byrd quickly told Bennett. With its engine still leaking oil, the plane banked and flew steadily into the bright light. Byrd stuck his head out the trapdoor, the Arctic blast burning his face. Peering through his amber goggles, he checked the sun compass. A shadow fell across it, proving his calculations were correct and that they were right on track.

"Surely fate was good to us," Byrd said, "for without the sun our quest of the Pole would have been hopeless."

By 4:30 p.m. on May 9 in a cloudless sky, Byrd and Bennett safely landed their plane in Spitsbergen. It took them fifteen and a half hours to fly to the North Pole and back. His crew cheered and threw their hats in the air. Igloo barked as he ran as fast as he could toward Byrd.

Byrd reached down and petted Igloo's brown ears. "Hello, Igloo," he said. "We're going home soon. You'll be glad to hear that, won't you?"

Two days later, on May 11, Byrd asked Igloo if he wanted to fly. Igloo hopped into the Fokker airplane without a second thought. The engines roared to life, and the plane raced down the runway, taking off like a bird into the air. Soon after, Amundsen's dirigible lifted into the sunny sky and followed.

Igloo, Byrd, and Bennett were leading the way on the first leg of Amundsen's journey to the North Pole. Igloo coolly patrolled the cabin while Bennett and Byrd piloted and navigated the plane. Three days later, Amundsen landed his dirigible in Point Barrow, Alaska, after also successfully flying over the North Pole.

Roald Amundsen (center with mustache and tie) stands in front of Byrd's plane with his dirigible in the background.

When the *Chantier*'s rusty anchor was hoisted out of the icy water to begin their journey back to America, Byrd turned to Bennett.

"Now we can fly the Atlantic," Byrd said, already beginning to plan a nonstop transatlantic flight from New York to Paris. It had been tried by others, but had ended in disaster.

"I hope you take me with you," Bennett replied.

"We go together," Byrd promised.

At the time, neither one knew that only one of them would make it.

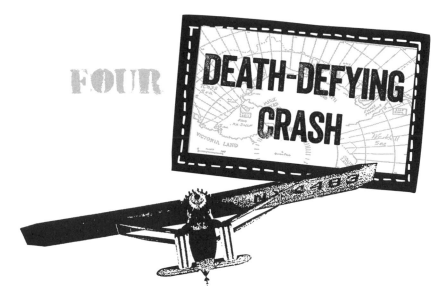

FOUR

DEATH-DEFYING CRASH

When Igloo left the land of the midnight sun, it wasn't the end of his life as an explorer. It was just the beginning. In fact, he would soon discover that his life was full of all kinds of discoveries. Igloo settled into his life on board the ship on his return to New York, and with the excitement of the North Pole flight behind him, everything else almost seemed humdrum. Igloo spent much of his free time playing with his stuffed toy goat.

One highlight of the return trip across the Atlantic for Igloo was the excitement in the radio room. Once the news of Byrd and Bennett's flight over the North Pole made headlines all over the world, the two men were international heroes. The president of the United States, Calvin Coolidge, wired his congratulations over the radio. In fact, the radio on the ship was lit up and abuzz, and Igloo's friend Malcolm Hanson was busy fielding congratulatory radio messages nonstop.

When Byrd and Igloo arrived in New York on the morning of June 22, 1926, it was all-out pandemonium. The crowds were cheering wildly, waving flags and hats. It was an earsplitting welcome home, as airplanes flew overhead, ships blew whistles, and fireboats sprayed water like geysers. New York City even closed all of the schools, declaring it a holiday.

With the traffic stopped, Igloo soon found himself in a parade going up Broadway to City Hall. He tried to stay near Byrd while the ticker-tape confetti fell all around them. The noise and mobs of people made Igloo shiver with fear. He didn't want to get separated from Byrd and get lost in the big city of New York.

Byrd was just as overwhelmed as Igloo by the response.

"All of this was entirely unexpected," Byrd wrote later. "I felt bewildered. But most grateful that the nation should do this for us."

And Byrd's hero's welcome was just beginning. After the parade, Igloo boarded a train with Byrd, and the pair traveled to Washington, DC. Technically, Igloo wasn't allowed on the train — no dogs were. But for Igloo, they made an exception. Once there, President Coolidge presented Byrd and Bennett with medals from the National Geographic Society. Byrd received the Hubbard medal, the highest award, and Bennett received a gold medal "for his distinguished service for flying to the North Pole" with Byrd.

Byrd and Bennett both received medals from President Coolidge (pictured giving Byrd his medal with Bennett to the right) for their flight over the North Pole.

After the president presented the medals, the crowd gradually fell silent. They were waiting for him to speak. Byrd's face turned pale. He was not used to speaking in front of thousands of people, and it was an imposing crowd — full of influential political leaders. Pushing his fear aside, he spoke up. At first, his voice was low, but it soon gained strength.

"In accepting this medal, I cannot but feel that I am representing the half hundred members of our expedition. I was only one of them. So in their behalf and for our expedition's sponsors, I want to express our very deep appreciation for this great honor."

Soon after, Byrd and Igloo arrived in Boston, Massachusetts, the city where Byrd lived when he wasn't exploring. They were driven to 9 Brimmer Street, a quiet street just around the corner from Charles Street and the Boston Common Frog Pond in Beacon Hill. Their suitcases were unloaded onto the sidewalk in front of a five-story, ivy-covered redbrick townhouse.

They walked up the steps to the front door and into Byrd's home. Once inside, one couldn't

Byrd and Igloo sitting on the front steps of their home at 9 Brimmer Street in Boston.

help but notice that the first-floor ceilings soared fourteen feet high, and the house was shaped like a giant slice of pie — wide at the front and narrow at the back.

But the biggest surprise for Igloo was that Byrd had a family — his wife, Marie, who Byrd had loved from the moment he met her when they were just kids in Virginia, and three children.

Igloo was introduced to Byrd's six-year-old, curly-haired son, Richard ("Dickie") Evelyn Byrd III; his four-year-old daughter, Evelyn ("Bolling"), who had strawberry blond hair; and his two-year-old daughter, Katherine.

Igloo also learned that Byrd had two brothers. Harry, Byrd's older brother, was the governor of Virginia, and Byrd's younger brother, Tom, was one of the largest apple growers in Maryland. And when Igloo went through the not-so-secret passageways on the second and third floors in the back of the house, he would discover that it led him to Byrd's father-in-law's home.

Byrd's family was delighted to make Igloo's acquaintance, and the children were eager to be friends with him. Surprisingly, though, Igloo felt shy. He'd never been around children before, and he decided to stick close by Byrd's side.

Like Byrd's schedule, Igloo's was very full. Igloo's day began very early every morning. Once awake, Igloo would rest his head on his white paws and watch Byrd sleep. Igloo was always extra careful to not make noise and disturb Byrd's slumber.

Once Byrd was awake, Igloo would snap to

attention and watch Byrd perform his morning calisthenics. Then Byrd got dressed and was ready to accompany Igloo into the walnut-paneled dining room. While there, Igloo would watch the fish swim in a gigantic aquarium sitting in the bay window, and Byrd would read the newspaper while they ate breakfast together. Afterward, Byrd and Igloo walked up the staircase to the second floor and into the study. There was a cozy fireplace with bookshelves built around it, and a large globe stood next to the desk where Byrd sat and worked. He had thousands of letters to respond to, books to work on, lectures to give, people to meet, and money to raise for the adventures he was planning.

Igloo curled up contentedly by Byrd's feet and waited quietly until he was finished. One of the best times of day for Igloo was when he and Byrd took a brisk walk along the Charles River Esplanade. It was during these walks that Byrd would think about plans for his next adventure and Igloo would occasionally find himself chasing squirrels.

But like the candy Igloo couldn't resist — Igloo

had the uncanny ability to hear crinkling candy wrappers at great distances — the children's madcap games and adventures proved to be irresistible. Byrd's housekeeper, Norah, who was a strict disciplinarian, said Igloo "caused more trouble than a dozen children."

But if Byrd ever happened to walk into the room while Igloo was in the midst of playing, Igloo would stop suddenly and act very serious and dignified, as if he hadn't playing at all. Igloo was a professional explorer, after all, with a reputation at stake. And he and Byrd had a lot of work to do if Byrd was going to be the first to fly nonstop across the Atlantic.

In the spring of 1927, the ongoing race to be the first to fly an airplane nonstop from New York to Paris had heated up. Raymond Orteig, a Frenchmen who had made a name for himself as a top-notch restaurateur and hotelier in New York, became interested in aviation during World War I, when countless aviators stayed at his hotel. In 1919, he offered a $25,000 prize to the first person to succeed. Many attempts had been made, all ending in disaster — with two men burning to death in a fiery plane crash. In the summer of 1927 alone, thirty people would die trying to make the trip.

Byrd wasn't interested in the prize money. In fact, he never officially entered the contest. At the time, little was known about flying long distances with heavy loads. And if Byrd could successfully fly across the Atlantic in a heavy trimotor plane, then he could prove that commercial oceanic flights were not only possible but practical, thereby opening the doors for the development of an airline industry. So Byrd packed his bags, and he and Igloo headed for New York, the starting point for the race to fly nonstop over the Atlantic.

For this flight, Byrd again carefully chose his airplane, a Fokker trimotor, and helped design some special features, paying particular attention to safety. One special feature was a safety valve Byrd developed. If the plane was about to crash, a valve could be pulled to dump the gasoline from the engines and prevent a fire. Byrd's copilot on the flight, Floyd Bennett, requested a switch that would shut down the three engines all at once if a crash landing was unavoidable. Byrd and Bennett also had catwalks added to the outside of the plane so they could fix mechanical problems mid-flight — they would just have to hang on tight.

With a crew of four, eight hundred pounds of emergency supplies and equipment, eight hundred gallons of gasoline in the tank alone, and radio equipment, the plane was heavy. So Byrd had a specially designed runway built at Roosevelt Field on Long Island, New York. The runway was longer and built down a hill. The downward slope allowed the plane to reach a faster speed for takeoff.

It was late in the afternoon at the Teterboro Airport near Hasbrouck Heights, New Jersey, on April 20, 1927, when Igloo watched Byrd climb into his recently built plane, *America*. Byrd was accompanying Anthony Fokker, the designer of the plane and vice president of the Atlantic Aircraft Corporation, on its first test flight.

Also along for the ride were Byrd's crew members for the transatlantic crossing. Floyd Bennett was in the cockpit next to Fokker, who was at the controls. Behind them, Byrd was standing in the navigator's cockpit next to the broad-shouldered George Noville. Noville, who had been with Byrd on the North Pole expedition, was going to operate the radio and fill in as a relief pilot on the crossing.

The sky was hazy when the plane took off. It soared into the sky and everything was running smoothly. The flight was perfect — until they tried to land. That's when Byrd saw Bennett lick his lips.

"This is the only sign Bennett gives when he is nervous — which I may say, is very rare," said Byrd.

When Fokker cut the engines to bring it in for a landing, the plane took a nosedive at a breakneck speed. Fokker yanked the throttle, pulling the plane back up into the air. He looked back at Byrd.

They knew the outlook was grim. There was too much weight in the front of the plane, and the fuel tank, which was running on empty, was blocking Byrd and Noville from the back of the plane. There was no way to distribute the weight and balance the plane.

"We've got to come down anyway," said Byrd.

Byrd and Noville crouched down, holding on to the seats in front of them. Fokker cut the throttle, and the plane's two front wheels touched the ground. Fokker opened the trapdoor overhead, and was flung headfirst out of the plane. The plane sped along the runway, kicking up dust, as the tail of the plane kept rising, higher and higher. Suddenly, the plane went over its nose. The center propeller was ripped off, and the front end of the plane was smashed in like an accordion as the plane somersaulted and landed on its back.

Igloo felt sheer panic in his heart, and he tore across the runway.

Inside, Byrd, Bennett, and Noville were trapped. Byrd's arm had snapped like a dry twig from the impact.

"Look out for fire!" cried Bennett weakly.

Everyone was worried that a fire would break out and they would burn alive. Noville, who was in terrible pain from internal injuries, frantically tore a hole through the fabric walls of the fuselage. He climbed out, and Byrd followed.

Once on the ground, Byrd looked for Bennett. He heard a cry from the plane, and rushed back inside.

Bennett was still trapped in his pilot's seat, hanging upside down. He'd received the full force of the impact from the crash when an engine slammed into him. There were two big gashes on his head. His face was covered in blood and his body was drenched in oil. His leg was broken above his knee, his right shoulder was dislocated, and a rib was broken. The pain was so bad he was barely conscious.

"Guess I'm done for," said Bennett. "I'm all broken up. I can't see and I have no feeling in my left arm."

Byrd tried to reassure him, not wanting to let on that things looked bad. Very bad. With one hand, Byrd wiped the blood and oil out of Bennett's eyes. Others came and helped Byrd cut Bennett free.

Everyone was rushed to the hospital. On the way, Byrd grimaced as he set his own broken arm.

The next time Igloo saw Byrd, his arm was in a sling and the worry lines in his face had deepened. But Byrd was relieved that Bennett had miraculously survived the crash. When Byrd saw Igloo, he couldn't help but smile.

"It might have been worse, Igloo," said Byrd. "We're going to try again. We're going to rebuild the plane and we'll be in Paris before long."

Byrd and Bennett check out the plane, *America*, after it is fixed and ready to go.

Igloo moved closer to Byrd. Then he gently licked Byrd's hand.

Byrd's next attempt came more than two months later on June 29, 1927. Although Charles "Lucky Lindy" Lindbergh had already successfully crossed the Atlantic in a single engine plane all by himself, Byrd's enthusiasm had not waned despite the fact that Bennett wouldn't be flying with him.

Bennett was still in the hospital. His right leg was in a cast, and his left leg was braced with steel splints and bandages. Nevertheless, he would be with Byrd and his crew the whole way — listening for bulletins on the radio by his hospital bed.

Replacing Bennett as the copilot was mustached Bert Acosta, a renowned stunt flier and naval

Byrd getting sworn in as a mail carrier by the U.S. Post Office. Byrd would deliver the first batch of transatlantic "air mail."

reserve officer. The other copilot was Norwegian Bernt Balchen, who had helped Byrd fix his plane's skis for Byrd's North Pole flight. Balchen could also fly an airplane by just using the instruments, which was invaluable.

George Noville, who had recovered from his injuries, had an extremely important job on the flight. As the radio operator, he would be communicating with the steamships on the Atlantic Ocean. The steamships would transmit the weather reports to him, which would help Byrd navigate along the way.

For weeks, the weather, which was critical to their success, hadn't been cooperating. Constant rain and fog had delayed their departure date.

At 1 a.m. on June 29, 1927, Byrd had only been asleep for an hour when he and Igloo were startled awake by the telephone ringing. It was the weather bureau. Byrd was told the weather was as good as it would get. Byrd quickly phoned his crew. By dawn, Byrd and his crew were ready for takeoff.

In the drizzling rain, Igloo was standing near Tom, Byrd's younger brother, as he watched the plane speed down the runway. When the plane

Byrd and his flight crew. From left to right: Bert Acosta, Byrd, George Noville, and Bernt Balchen.

lifted into the air, Tom heard a "half-choked sound, almost like a cry" from Igloo. Igloo tugged on his leash, trying to break free. It was only when the plane was high in the sky that Igloo finally stopped pulling.

With Byrd gone, Igloo was miserable. It

wasn't until later, when he caught a glimpse of a woodchuck and chased it at full speed that Igloo felt his spirits lift.

Up in the air, just north of Halifax, Canada, Byrd looked through the plane's trapdoor. He saw a beautiful bright rainbow, and it seemed to be moving with the plane.

"I could not help but think it was an augury of a good omen," said Byrd.

But that was wishful thinking.

For the next forty-two hours the rain and fog were relentless.

"We were lost several times," said Byrd. "But I always knew approximately where we were."

They flew their plane at a high altitude, which usually kept them out of the fog and clouds. But even at higher altitudes, they were forced to fly through enormous clouds. This was dangerous since ice could form on the plane's wings, causing the plane to fall out of the sky.

"During the dark hours when I was working on my charts," said Byrd, "I could tell when we were in a thick cloud by the water dripping into the navigator's cabin."

With the persistent fog and clouds, Byrd and his crew were forced to fly blind for nineteen hours. That is, they flew without seeing land, water, or a clear sky.

"We did not find it a very agreeable sensation," said Byrd.

But Balchen's skill at instrument flying was a lifesaver. Even so, by the time they reached the fog-covered Paris, their compasses went out, fuel was low, and they needed to find a place to land — soon. When Byrd looked out the window, it was as dark as black ink.

Byrd had to make a decision, and it was do-or-die.

"In the confusion of the storm, we were afraid we might run out of gas and have to land in the dark and perhaps kill someone, not to speak of ourselves," said Byrd.

Byrd knew what they had to do. He signaled to Balchen, who was piloting the plane, to circle back to the coastal village of Ver-sur-Mer, near Normandy. Once there, Byrd dropped flares out of the trapdoor. When they hit the water, the flares illuminated the ocean beneath them. For a few short minutes, there would be light.

With only one choice left, Balchen circled the plane around the light and descended, hurtling toward the ocean.

"It was amazing the force of the water as we hit," said Byrd. "It sheared off the landing gear . . . as if it had been of straw . . . then the bottom of the fuselage ripped open and the plane filled with water instantly."

Byrd shot out a window. He had been hit in the chest, and his heart was thumping. He swam over to where he thought he heard Noville shouting his name. Byrd called out, but they were all having trouble hearing. The constant roar of the engines had their ears ringing.

Through the darkness, Byrd could faintly see Noville climb out a window. Relieved that Noville appeared to be okay, Byrd swam to the cockpit. He reached in and found Balchen, who was dazed but in the process of freeing himself. Byrd grabbed Balchen by the back of his neck and pulled him out of the plane.

Byrd yelled at the top of his lungs for Acosta. There was no answer. They looked through the window into the cabin but there was no one there. Byrd noticed the wing of the plane was underwater

The plane after the crash landing in the ocean.

and so was the fuselage. He feared the worst —
that Acosta was trapped underwater. They yelled
and yelled for him. But there was no reply.

They were treading in the cold water, with
darkness surrounding them, when Acosta
suddenly appeared — alive and well despite a
broken collarbone.

"Believe me," said Byrd. "I was the happiest
man in the world."

When Byrd finally returned to 9 Brimmer
Street — after receiving a second ticker-tape
parade in New York for his transatlantic flight —

Igloo was overjoyed to see him. He had missed Byrd terribly. Since he couldn't tell Byrd how happy he was to see him again, he decided to show him.

Igloo went into the living room, where there was a table and chair that was once owned by Napoleon. Byrd kept his charts and maps from the North Pole on the table, and Igloo stored his toy goat under Napoleon's chair. Without hesitating, Igloo grabbed his beloved stuffed toy goat and went back over to Byrd. Igloo looked up at Byrd and dropped his toy goat at Byrd's feet, giving Byrd his most precious belonging.

Byrd responded in kind.

"Would you like to go for a walk, Igloo?"

It was exactly what Igloo wanted to hear. There was nothing Igloo wanted more — being with Byrd was his most favorite thing in the whole world.

It wasn't long after that that a worrisome thought crept into Igloo's mind. He learned that Byrd was making plans to go to the Antarctic to fly across the South Pole, which had never been done before.

The Antarctic is the coldest, driest, windiest, and iciest place in the world, with normal temperatures well below freezing. At the time, very little was known about the continent.

"The ice-barrier, the frightful weather, and the lack of animal life are a few of the things that have hampered exploration," said Byrd. "Taken together they form almost insuperable obstacles."

But Byrd knew one thing for sure. Flying to the South Pole would be more treacherous than flying to the North Pole.

While Byrd spent hours planning for his most dangerous feat yet, Igloo was worried — worried that he would be left behind. After all, he didn't get to fly across the Atlantic. But Igloo had a plan.

In the meantime, Byrd chose Bennett to be second-in-command on the expedition to Antarctica. Even though Bennett was still weak from his injuries from the crash, he had happily taken care of nearly half of their preparations.

"Everything that has to do with transportation is in his hands," said Byrd. "And I do not have to worry about it."

Bennett, whose nerves were still like steel, tested the three planes they were taking on the trip. Bennett even flew the big Ford trimotor plane, which Byrd planned to fly over the South Pole, in northern Canada where the temperature was thirty-five degrees below zero.

But four months before the first ship was to set sail to Antarctica, Bennett piloted a rescue flight to save the lives of four marooned flyers who had set out to fly across the Atlantic, but were forced to crash-land on Greenly Island in Canada.

The 1,500-mile flight in subzero temperatures proved to be too much for Bennett's weakened condition. Several days later Bennett died from pneumonia with Byrd at his bedside. Byrd was grief stricken.

"Bennett was one of the coolest and bravest men I ever knew," said Byrd. "He was a man of the greatest energy, endurance, and skill, both as a navigator and as a mechanic."

After the sudden death of his trusted friend, the Antarctic expedition almost didn't happen. But it soon took on a new meaning for Byrd.

"I intend to go through with the Antarctic expedition as a memorial to Floyd Bennett," Byrd announced in a message. "I shall name the Antarctic plane to be used in an attempt to fly over the Pole *Floyd Bennett*."

But it would never be the same without Bennett.

"Hundreds were the times I was to feel his loss," said Byrd.

On the day of Byrd's departure, Igloo knew it was time to put his well-thought-out plan into action. First, he was on his very best behavior. Second, he kept a close eye on Byrd, never leaving his side, following him up and down the staircase, while Byrd piled his suitcases near the front door. Finally, when Byrd set the last one down, Igloo planted himself firmly by the tower of suitcases. Mission accomplished.

When the taxi arrived, Igloo watched Byrd and his family hug and kiss. It was a tearful good-bye. It would be years before he would see them again — if he survived. The *New York Times* newspaper had already written an obituary for every person going on the expedition, expecting someone — if not all of them — to die.

Byrd opened the car door and took a seat. Then he turned and shouted, "Hop in, Igloo! We're in a hurry."

Igloo's heart soared, and he leaped onto Byrd's lap. As the taxi sped away, Igloo looked out the

Byrd and Igloo on their journey to the bottom of the world.

window and barked enthusiastically. He and Byrd were once again on a great adventure, together, headed to the bottom of the world.

FIVE

TO THE BOTTOM OF THE WORLD

After a long train ride from New York to California — which ran behind schedule when Igloo decided to take off and chase a gopher — Igloo found himself with Byrd on a steel whaling ship, the *C.A. Larsen*. Their oceanic journey began when they set sail from the Port of Los Angeles on October 10, 1928. For the first leg of the 10,000-mile trip to the bottom of the world, it was smooth sailing for Igloo.

The *Larsen* was one of three ships that Byrd was using to haul the men, supplies, equipment, and three airplanes to the Antarctic. The other two, the *Eleanor Bolling* (named after Byrd's mom, who was also the namesake of Byrd's oldest daughter) and the *City of New York*, had left from different ports. The three ships planned to meet in New Zealand to resupply, refuel, and reload before embarking on the last leg of the journey — the most dangerous part — through the maze of menacing ice.

Igloo felt right at home on the *Larsen*, and as always, he had full run of the ship. But after his first once-over below deck, he steadfastly refused to go down below again. No matter what Byrd said to try to convince him otherwise, Igloo kept his distance.

Byrd suspected that the cow, which was brought along to supply fresh milk and was living down below, might be the reason Igloo refused. That may have been true, but there may have been another very good reason, too.

While Byrd was busy, checking the supply lists, making plans, and discussing the ice conditions with the captain, sometimes for several hours, Igloo was very busy, too.

Igloo's favorite pastime on board the *Larsen* was hiding under Byrd's deck chair on the main deck of the ship. Like a lion stalking his prey,

Igloo crouched down on his haunches and waited patiently for just the right moment. Then, when he spotted a crew member who was unwittingly walking by Byrd's chair, Igloo suddenly shot out from under it.

Feigning an attack, Igloo barked savagely and enjoyed scaring the living daylights out of the unsuspecting sailor. Nonetheless, Igloo always wagged his tail at him, letting him know it was all in good fun — albeit at his expense.

"Neither modesty nor humility, I regret to say, was in his attitude," said Byrd.

However, Igloo was always very careful to avoid pulling his prank on the officers. He knew how to spot them. The high-ranking officers wore lots of brass buttons. In fact, whenever Igloo was in an officer's presence, or in the presence of anyone who had authority, he was always "the very picture of innocence."

But Igloo's fun and games came to an abrupt halt on December 2, 1928. This was the day he and Byrd set sail on the *City of New York* for the second leg of their journey. And when Igloo went out for a stroll on the poop deck toward the back of the ship, he finally met his match.

The *City of New York* was old and slow, but it wasn't an ordinary steamship. It was an ice ship. And, unlike other steamships, the *City* had a V-shaped hull covered with tough and slippery wood. This helped lift the ship out of the water so it wasn't crushed by the ice. The bow of the ship was outfitted with heavy steel plates, and the sides of the ship, which were three-feet thick, were reinforced with cross timbers to prevent it from being crushed by the ice.

Although the *City* was one of the larger ice ships, it was jam-packed and overflowing with all of the supplies Byrd was taking to the Antarctic. Igloo was overwhelmed by the mountainous piles of boxes and crates towering over him, threatening to topple over. But there was a lot to bring on the expedition.

There were eighty-three men on the three ships, and forty-one men who would be staying with Byrd in the Antarctic. With so many mouths to feed, a lot of planning went in to the supply of food, which is scarce in the Antarctic. Plants did not grow there, and animals, such as seals, penguins, and whales, were the only source of meat along the coast. Farther inland there was no food at all.

The task of creating a food budget, buying the food, and planning menus fell on the shoulders of Igloo's good friend Cook Tennant; oval-faced Sidney Greason, the chief steward on the expedition; and Dr. Francis Coman, the expedition's physician, who Igloo would soon know quite well.

"It's quite a job to know just what and how much food to take on for two years," said Cook Tennant.

They paid particular attention to how the food was packaged. It couldn't be stored in heavy, breakable glass jars. And it couldn't be stored in tin cans. The cold temperatures cause glass jars to burst and tin to become brittle. A noncorrosive metal, such as a nickel-copper alloy, would have to be used. Plastic was not considered since it hadn't been invented yet.

Greason, who had fifteen years of experience as a butcher, did not skimp on quality and personally picked out every ham and turkey himself.

"I'm buying the best. . . . If I have any claim to distinction, it is that I know good food, and that I get it," he said.

As a result, there were twenty-five tons of chicken, turkey, beef, ham, hot dogs, and bacon to haul to the Antarctic, 2,500 pounds of pemmican, 2,000 pounds of cocoa, and 3,000 pounds of powdered milk, not to mention loads of canned and dehydrated fruits and vegetables.

Enormous amounts of flour were also purchased so bread, rolls, and pies could be baked every day. They also bought large quantities of birthday candles so everyone's birthday could be properly celebrated.

"No man . . . is going to have a chance to sigh for home cooking or for pies like Mother used to make," said Greason, "because he is going to have them all while he is gone. Change of scenery is going to mean no change of food."

While the crew was busy loading and stacking all of these crates, Igloo knew to stay out of the way while he explored the ship. When he made his way down the stairs and into the forecastle, or fo'c's'le, which was in the front of the ship and where the crew's quarters were located, Igloo's body suddenly stiffened and he twitched his nose. He had caught a whiff of the musty, stale air that was damp from the saltwater and thick from tobacco smoke. The odor was unpleasant, but it didn't deter him.

Through the darkened hallway, weaving in and out of crates, Igloo passed by the cramped rooms filled with wooden bunk beds and overflowing with personal belongings and gear.

When Igloo made his way to the aft, or back of the ship, there were piles and piles of animal furs. On the expedition, each person would wear a fur snowsuit. And the person in charge of sewing all of the polar clothes was sixty-eight-year-old Norwegian sail maker, Martin Ronne. The suspender-wearing Ronne was the oldest person on the expedition and the only one who had ever been to the Antarctic before — back in 1911, when Amundsen was the first person to set foot on the South Pole. Amundsen had recommended him to Byrd because Ronne was not only the best sail maker in the polar-exploring business; he was also the best tailor of polar clothes.

Igloo could always find Ronne sitting busily behind his sewing machine making fur parkas, pants, boots, sleeping bags, tents, and sails. Ronne could sew it all, paying particular attention to the type of fur and the size. Although Byrd brought along the polar-bear-fur pants that he wore to the North Pole, Ronne was making the crew's pants out of caribou skin with the fur side facing out. Inside they were lined with fawn or squirrel skin.

"In making up all these garments the rule must be remembered that fur outside keeps the cold out, and fur inside keeps the warmth in," said Byrd.

The boots were of utmost importance. Sweaty feet were a big problem, and sweat will freeze, causing frostbite. In the Antarctic, it's easy to lose toes to frostbite, especially when temperatures reach seventy-five degrees below zero.

To solve this serious problem, Ronne made the boot bigger. A bigger boot gave room for at least two pairs of socks — one made out of caribou skin and the other made out of wool.

To wick moisture away from the socks, the boots were stuffed with a dry, haylike grass called *senna* from the foot of the boot to halfway to the top. The final problem to work out was that the jagged ice wore the boots out quickly. Sealskin, which is tough and waterproof, was used on the soles of the boots to fix this problem. The upper part of the boot was made of caribou skin.

Like the boots, the gloves were made of caribou and sealskin and were oversized so wool mittens could fit inside. The sleeping bags were also made of caribou skin.

Along with the fur snowsuits, the men needed to bring skis, ski boots made of kangaroo hide, ski suits, windbreakers, long underwear, and sun goggles. And since the crew would have to provide their own entertainment during the long, dark winter days, they also packed plenty of musical instruments, like ukuleles, banjos, guitars, saxophones, and even a piano.

Igloo could always find Martin Ronne busy at his sewing machine.

Unlike the men, Igloo had packed lightly. He'd just brought along his new favorite toy — a little rubber ball with the face of a cat on one side of it. He loved the way it squeaked when he squeezed it because it sounded like a "meow."

As Igloo continued to explore the ship, it wasn't long before he found himself on the poop deck. And it was there that he was about to lose something very important to him.

As Igloo wandered along the dirt-covered deck and through the piles of gear and boxes, something caught his eye. Dozens of wooden crates with wire mesh doors were scattered and anchored all around the poop deck and on top of the gigantic crate that contained Byrd's Ford airplane, the one he planned to fly over the South Pole.

Igloo's nose twitched. There was a familiar scent in the air. Curious, Igloo walked over to investigate, looking through the mesh wire and into the dark crate. This was a big mistake.

A giant dog with ferocious-looking fangs hurled his massive body against the mesh wire, barking wildly and trying to attack Igloo. Suddenly, there was vicious growling and barking all around him, as the Eskimo sled dogs tried to free themselves, hoping to rip Igloo to shreds.

Igloo's body trembled, shaking uncontrollably with fear. His brown-green eyes flashed wildly around as he tried to decide what to do. His white tail went up in a friendly manner, and then it went down in surrender. Up. Down. Up. Down.

Igloo quickly came to his senses and ran with his tail between his legs as fast as he could — only to find more dogs leashed to the ships railing, straining and rattling their chains, fangs snarling trying to sink their teeth into Igloo as he flew by.

Igloo kept running. And running. And running. He never slowed down, not even when he was safely below deck. He ran at top speed through the fo'c's'le, and kept on running and running.

When Igloo finally had a chance to collect himself, he realized he'd lost something very important up on the poop deck — he had lost his courage.

"Until this trip," said Byrd, "I fancied neither man nor beast could discompose him. He met his superiors, however, in the Eskimo dogs, and in admitting to himself their superiority, his spirit underwent an extraordinary change. He hardly dared venture on deck alone. . . . Poor Igloo, I did not blame him. Those huge creatures would assassinate him on the spot, as he was shrewd enough to realize."

And Byrd was shrewd enough to realize that sled dogs were critical to the survival of the men on the expedition. Their job was to haul the supplies over the snow, ice, and deadly crevasses to the campsite where the crew would be busy building underground houses for shelter.

The most famous sled dog on the expedition was Chinook, who was part Eskimo husky and part mutt. He was big, at one hundred pounds, with a golden coat of fur and silver muzzle. Chinook's grandfather had been Robert Peary's lead sled dog when he discovered the North Pole in 1909. Chinook was considered the world's greatest sled dog of all time, having won one of the first international sled dog races in 1922.

Chinook's driver, the grizzled Arthur Walden, was considered the best sled-dog driver in the country. Part of their success together was their deep bond of love and respect for each other.

"He is eleven years old and the greatest leader I have ever known," Walden said about Chinook.

"We will keep him reserved to take the lead in case of emergencies. Nothing can stop him."

Although Byrd was bringing the most cutting-edge technology with him to the Antarctic, he knew that mechanical equipment was prone to failing in extremely cold weather. But sled dogs were tried and true and had been proven to be the most reliable transportation in the Antarctic.

"Dogs you see, are the only animal to use down there," said Walden. "The dog doesn't sweat, so he can do hard work and then lie right down on the

The sled dogs on deck. Their howling kept Igloo up at night while he tried to sleep in Byrd's quarters directly below.

ice and sleep. He doesn't need water, and he can go five days without food and still do hard work."

Even so, Igloo didn't like the sled dogs one bit. They terrified him. And it didn't help that night after night, the sled dogs threw their heads back and howled a mournful, eerie moan. It would start with one howl and then the other dogs would join in.

While the dogs howled, directly below them, in Byrd and Igloo's room, Igloo couldn't sleep. Haunted, he shivered with fear and hid behind a box and under his blanket. It wasn't until the howling stopped that he risked coming out. But the howling soon got worse.

Fierce storms rolled in and brutal waves soaked the men and dogs as the ship rolled dangerously back and forth and up and down. Unhappy, the sled dogs howled all day and night.

As the days passed, the nights grew shorter as the summer months approached the Southern Hemisphere. The stormy weather subsided, but the ship was soon dodging icebergs, and by December 15, there was thick ice everywhere. The ship had reached the pack ice.

Breaking through the thick ice pack without

sinking is tricky. The *Bolling* had already turned around to go back to New Zealand because it had been unable to break through the ice.

The *City* couldn't make it through the pack ice on its own, either. It didn't have enough engine power. So the crew used a three-and-a-half-inch thick wire cable that was attached to the *Larsen* and the *City*. Taking the lead, the *Larsen* cautiously pushed her bow against the ice and then lurched forward at full speed, breaking through. As the *Larsen* sped ahead, it pulled the *City* through the watery opening. The noise from the breaking ice was so deafening as to be almost unbearable.

"Down below, in the fo'c's'le, it is like standing in a chamber the walls of which are being pounded with giant hammers," said Byrd. "There would come an impact, the deck would tilt alarmingly, then the ship would sag with groaning timbers and the shriek of cracking ice would sound outside."

When the ice broke apart, there was a period of calm as the ship was pulled through, and it was during this time, two days later, when Igloo cautiously went up onto the main deck — keeping his distance from the sled dogs.

Igloo tried to tune out the barking sled dogs

and enjoy himself. After all, Cook Tennant had made him roast lamb for lunch, and he was feeling pretty good. He stationed himself near a trusted crew member and knew Byrd wasn't far away. He was busy in the chart room. Igloo gazed out at the endless barren ice when he caught a glimpse of something moving.

He got up from his spot and scurried over to the railing to get a better look. But there was nothing there. Then he saw something move again. And it was coming right toward him.

Waddling on the ice and coming right up to the side of the ship was a three-foot-tall emperor penguin. Igloo stood up on his hind legs, his two front paws resting on the railing. He looked hard at the black-and-white penguin with bright yellow ear patches. Igloo barked at it happily. Then the emperor penguin disappeared among the ice.

The ship once again began hammering through the ice when Igloo saw two small Adélie penguins pop up onto the ice. They tilted their heads to their sides, waved their flippers, and shuffled toward the ship. Igloo was beside himself, and he ran up and down the deck, barking.

"There was great hilarity aboard for awhile,"

Three-foot-tall emperor penguins.

said Byrd. "These comical creatures came to us unafraid, with friendly waves of flippers, tobogganing with great speed on their bellies across ice floes."

Some of the crew jumped off the ship onto the ice to play with the penguins. Igloo tried to jump off, too. But his plan was thwarted when someone grabbed his collar before he could join in on the fun. Nevertheless, as long as the Adélie penguins were nearby, Igloo didn't take his eyes off of them.

Soon the ice became slushy like thick soup, and Igloo and Byrd were on the open water in the Ross Sea. The *Larsen* was no longer needed to pull the *City* through the ice pack, so it turned around to go hunting for whales, leaving Byrd, Igloo, and the crew aboard the *City* to fend for themselves.

Two days later, on Christmas Day, there was a shout from high above in the ship's crow's nest: "Barrier on the starboard bow!"

Some of the crew were eating, and quickly pushed their plates aside. Everyone ran to the upper deck, eager for a better look at the mysterious Ross Ice Shelf, the largest floating body of glacier ice in the world.

With its towering, spiky wall and overhanging ice cliffs, it looked blue when the light from the sun fell on it. This was the place where Byrd and Igloo and the rest of crew would be living for the next year. And it was also the place where Igloo was about to rediscover his courage.

SIX

DOG DAYS

JANUARY 1929, ANTARCTICA

Igloo listened to the sounds of dogs barking, men shouting, and ice cracking. The noise pierced the deep, ever-present Antarctic silence. Once the ship had reached the recess in front of the Ross Ice Shelf, called the Bay of Whales, the crew hammered two-hundred-pound ice anchors into the solid pack ice, mooring the ship.

Not long after, Byrd found a spot where they would build their winter base, which he dubbed "Little America." The base was nine miles from the ship, which was a long distance to haul their supplies, especially with the constant threat of

Unloading the ship while the dogs and sleds stand by to haul the supplies away.

hidden ice crevasses. A fall into a crevasse by a crew member or dog would most likely be fatal. But it was important that the base was far enough away from the bay in case the ice broke off and floated out to sea.

Byrd and his team had their work cut out for them. Unloading and moving the supplies was a grueling, nonstop task that exhausted everyone. It would take months to complete, and they had to be finished before winter came and the sun disappeared for four months.

At the North and South Poles, there are two seasons, winter and summer, and they begin and end at opposite times. In the Southern Hemisphere, where the South Pole is located, the winter season begins near the end of March and lasts until the end of September, unlike in the Northern Hemisphere, where the North Pole is located, and where winter begins near the end of September and lasts until the end of March. This has to do with the tilt of the Earth's axis. In December, the Northern Hemisphere is tilted away from the sun, making it colder. But the Southern Hemisphere it tilted toward the sun, making it warmer.

For weeks now, Igloo and the penguins, groups of which were always nearby, watched the steady

The sled dogs were essential to the success of Byrd's Antarctic expedition, helping to haul supplies so the men could build Little America.

stream of boxes, crates, and barrels of supplies making their way down the wooden planks. Once the supplies were off the ship, they were hauled to Little America, a job that fell on the sled dogs.

As the sled dogs stepped off the ship and onto the ice for the first time, finally free from their cages, they were wildly excited, rolling in the snow, running in circles, and sometimes pouncing at one another's throats. Nevertheless, they were always eager to start work, trotting to their places, waiting to be harnessed.

The sled dogs and their drivers settled into their new home at Little America. The dogs slept in crates or buried themselves in the snow — with the exception of Chinook, who slept in a tent with Walden. Every morning after a quick cup of coffee, the sled-dog drivers cracked their whips and yelled *yake!* for straight ahead, *gee!* to turn right, *haw!* to turn left, and *whoa!* to slow down. Soon after, they would arrive at the ship to haul more supplies back to Little America. And whenever the dogs were nearby, Igloo was on full alert.

Igloo knew that if he kept out of their way, the sled dogs left him alone. He always paid close attention to when the dogs were harnessed to their wooden sleds, providing him with a little more security.

For safety, the ten-dog sled teams always worked in pairs. And someone always watched over them from the ship's crow's nest while they made two dangerous trips a day over shifting ice, running through the snow as fast as they could to Little America.

On January 17, Igloo and the others noticed that Chinook never arrived at the ship. This wasn't too unusual. Sometimes, he didn't lead the dogs when Walden didn't want him to get overworked. During those times, Chinook usually ran ahead or behind the sled, just to keep his eye on things. Whenever there was a difficult trail to follow, Walden could depend on Chinook.

But this time, Chinook had been running behind the team as they made their way toward the ship. He fell far behind, and when Walden looked, Chinook was nowhere to be seen. Some of the men were worried that Chinook had fallen into a crevasse.

"No," Walden said. He knew Chinook better than anyone. "Chinook was downed by three of the other dogs the day before and that means in a pack of husky dogs that he lost his leadership. He was never off his feet in a dog fight before. . . . He figured it all out. He was all through. And he came and bid me good-bye, but I didn't realize what he was doing until later. Then he walked off alone to find a place to die. . . . I dream of that dog yet. I can't get him out of my mind."

Like Igloo, the younger Adélie penguins also found the sled dogs interesting. But unlike Igloo, the penguins didn't know to keep a safe distance. Whenever the sled dogs were harnessed, waiting for the supplies to be loaded on their sleds, the penguins would make a dash toward them, waving their tiny wings.

The dogs waited patiently for the penguins to get close, and when they did, the dogs snapped and barked in attack. Many times Igloo witnessed penguins waddling away in pain, and sometimes the penguins had to be pulled from the dogs' clenched jaws, the snow red from their blood. Igloo tried to run interference to stop them, but the penguins always refused to listen.

Although Igloo kept his distance from the

dogs, he knew them from afar. There was Spy, a sled-dog leader. He was a big snow-white husky. His brothers, Watch and Moody, were part of his team. They were friendly to everyone, always holding out their paws, ready for a handshake. The brothers were devoted to one another, earning the nickname "the Three Musketeers."

There was also the plump husky dog named Moose-Moss-Mouse, so named because he looked like both a moose and mouse with a mossy coat. Moose-Moss-Mouse only had one eye, having lost the other in a fight. Some thought he was ugly, but his dog-team driver, Norwegian Chris Braathen, loved him and said that Moose-Moss-Mouse was "the best dog that ever was." Moose-Moss-Mouse's best friend was Tickle, a skinny but strong lead dog with black fur and a lot of pluck.

One day, while Igloo was busy doing his daily inspection around the ship, with no intention of making trouble, Tickle caught his eye. Igloo noticed Tickle and his team were harnessed securely to the sled. There was nothing unusual about that, but a thought suddenly occurred to Igloo, giving him an idea — one that he found not only foolproof but also irresistible.

Setting his sights on Tickle, Igloo charged at top speed right toward him and his team. When Igloo was just inches away, his plan was to veer away, wanting only to taunt Tickle. But the slippery ice betrayed him. And while he frantically tried to slow down, leaning back and dragging his rump across the ice, Igloo slid right into the middle of the pack of dogs.

The dogs immediately pounced on Igloo. They barked angrily, and Igloo's yelps for help could barely be heard buried beneath the ferocious growls. But Byrd heard him, and in a flash, he and Tickle's driver, George Thorne, rushed to the pileup of dogs. Using a whip and club, they broke up the fight. Byrd was sick with dread, fearing Igloo was at the bottom of the pile — dead.

But Igloo didn't have a single scratch. Everyone, including Igloo, was surprised. Igloo stood unsteadily on his tiny feet, shocked and shaking. He managed a slight upward glance at Byrd and a little wag of his tail. He didn't protest as Byrd led him back to the ship. Instead, Igloo stayed right next to Byrd. But Igloo had discovered something very important in the pileup, and he was certain the other dogs knew it, too. With Byrd by his side, Igloo was the top dog.

Byrd and Igloo in the Antarctic.

Buoyed by this thought, Igloo devised a new game that delighted him, but he only played it when the sled dogs were harnessed. Now, whenever the sled dogs ran by, pulling the heavily loaded sled, Igloo would run as fast as he could alongside them, but not close enough that they could reach him. His game made the dogs so angry that they would get tangled up in the harness, and sometimes the sled toppled over. It wasn't long before Igloo was no longer allowed near the sled dogs, much to his chagrin.

So Igloo shifted his attention to the penguins. He favored the smaller and friendlier Adélies over the emperors. Whenever he saw them, Igloo wagged his tail in a friendly wave and he greeted them with happy noises. He liked to line the Adélies up in a row and tackle them. It was fun until they started clobbering him with their wings.

When the penguins weren't up to playing games, Igloo enjoyed yanking the big gray Weddell seals' tails — that is, until Byrd reprimanded

Igloo meets a penguin.

him. But that didn't stop Igloo — from then on he always made sure no one was watching.

On Wednesday, January 30, the day came to unload the fuselage of Byrd's big Ford airplane, Igloo was on board the *City*, keeping a close eye on the activities. The *City* had been tied to the *Bolling*, which had returned with more supplies, and they were now anchored to the ice barrier that was as high as the ship's bridge.

A crane lifted the fuselage from the ship's hold, and it was carefully placed on the ice barrier. Soon after, the ships rocked, jolting the edge of the ice barrier. The ice barrier cracked in an explosion of sound as an avalanche of snow and ice, weighing hundreds of tons, fell into the ocean and onto both ships. The ships rolled dangerously, nearly capsizing.

Igloo slid willy-nilly across the tilted deck, only to be saved from going overboard by landing in the scupper, or drain.

But airplane mechanic Bennie Roth, who had been standing on the ice barrier, wasn't so lucky. He fell into the icy water and he didn't know how to swim. Sinking, he grabbed an ice floe, but it was too slippery and kept spinning. His numb hands couldn't hold it securely. Roth cried out for help as he reached for another ice floe.

Byrd, who had been in his cabin, ran up on to the deck, wearing only a gray flannel shirt and pants over his long underwear. He ran to the rail and jumped across the wide gap onto the *Bolling*. He scanned the ice-filled water for Roth.

"It seemed impossible to me that he could continue to hold on to that spinning ice," said Byrd.

His only thought was that he was responsible for Roth's life. Byrd knew he could reach him, and, without hesitating, Byrd plunged into the icy water to rescue Roth. But ice had floated between Byrd and Roth, blocking the way.

Byrd's entire body was immediately stiff and numb. The water was too cold to swim in and his legs were nearly immobile. Soon Byrd, too, was fighting to stay alive.

Roth was getting tired, struggling to keep his head above the water. His clothes were weighing him down, but he had managed to grab ahold of two ice floes, one under each arm. His clothes and hands were frozen fast to them. Stunned, he remained calm, but he shouted out that he couldn't hold on much longer.

A lifeboat was hurriedly dropped down ten feet into the water. As they paddled out to look for Roth, they came upon Byrd.

"Don't mind me," said Byrd. "I am all right. Go after Roth. He can't swim."

Byrd turned away and slowly swam toward the ship.

The rescue boat was having a hard time finding Roth. The sun was shining too brightly in their eyes. Luckily, the men on the ice barrier could see him, and they shouted and pointed. Finally the boat reached Roth. They pulled him into the boat. His body was so numb he landed in the boat face-first. They helped him sit up and wrapped him in blankets.

"I wasn't cold all over until I got out of the water," said Roth. "But then I couldn't move."

While the rescue boat made its way back, Byrd was close enough to the ship that a rope was dropped. He reached for it with his frozen hands and clung to it with all his might. The crew slowly pulled him up to the deck.

"Have they got Roth?" asked Byrd.

"Yes, he is all right."

"Thank God," said Byrd.

He and Roth were taken to the engine room to warm up, and it wasn't long after that Byrd was back on the deck overseeing the unloading of the supplies. The crew continued to work around the clock in subzero temperatures, brutal winds, and fierce snowstorms that were typical in the Antarctic. A few days later, all of the supplies were unloaded, and the ships set sail on February 22, leaving Byrd, Igloo, and forty-one men behind for the long winter ahead.

It was twenty-nine degrees below zero and time to move to Little America. Igloo had never been there before, but the sled dogs, who were

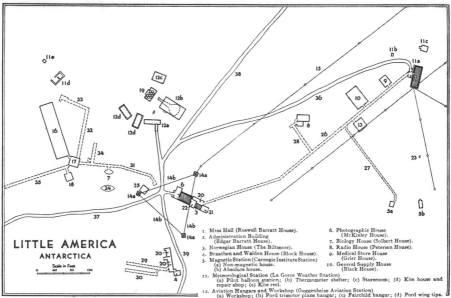

LITTLE AMERICA
ANTARCTICA

Scale in Feet
0   40   80   120

1. Mess Hall (Roswell Barratt House).
2. Administration Building (Edgar Barratt House).
3. Norwegian House (The Biltmore).
4. Braathen and Walden House (Block House).
5. Magnetic Station (Carnegie Institute Station)
   (a) Non-magnetic house.
   (b) Absolute house.
6. Photographic House (McKinley House).
7. Biology House (Solbert House).
8. Radio House (Petersen House).
9. Medical Store House (Grier House).
10. General Supply House (Black House).
11. Meteorological Station (La Gorce Weather Station)
   (a) Pilot balloon station; (b) Thermometer shelter; (c) Storeroom; (d) Kite house and repair shop; (e) Kite reel.
12. Aviation Hangars and Workshop (Guggenheim Aviation Station)
   (a) Workshop; (b) Ford trimotor plane hangar; (c) Fairchild hangar; (d) Ford wing tips.
13. Gymnasium (Fosdick Gymnasium). 14. Radio Station (Ochs Radio Station); (a) Towers; (b) Antennæ. 15. Antenna (Hanson Antenna). 16. Seal Cache. 17. Chopping House. 18. Maternity Ward. 19. Gasoline Cache. 20. Storerooms. 21. Coal Cache. 22. Machine Shop. 23. Radio Direction Finder. 24. Life Boat. 25. Snowmobile. 26. Main Tunnel (Lofgren Tunnel). 27. Magnetic Tunnel (Ronne Tunnel). 28. Fuel Tunnel (Bubier Tunnel). 29. Dog Tunnel (Walden Tunnel). 30. Dog Tunnel (Strom Tunnel). 31. Dog Tunnel (Parker Tunnel). 32. Dog Tunnel (Rucker Tunnel). 33. Dog Tunnel (June Tunnel). 34. Dog Tunnel (de Ganahl Tunnel). 35. Dog Tunnel (Van der Veer Tunnel). 36. Path between Administration Building and Mess Hall (Greason Street). 37. Trail to Bay (Finley Trail). 38. Trail to North (Carson Trail). 39. Trail to South (Grosvenor Trail).

busy pulling Igloo on the sled over the bay ice and around a cape, knew the way by heart. In an hour and a half, Igloo arrived and was ready to explore.

On the surface, there wasn't much to see of Little America, with the exception of the three radio towers with blinking lights and the stovepipes and ventilators. The rest of it was buried under the snow to help insulate against the cold.

Building Little America was one of the hardest jobs the crew undertook. Using shovels, the men dug down eight feet into concrete-hard ice. The uncomplaining carpenter, Chips Gould, who had been to the North Pole with Byrd, had to warm up the nails before hammering them into the orange prefab houses, otherwise the nails would break.

They built the Administration Building, the Mess Hall, and the Norwegian House (so named because the houses were from Norway). There was also a machine shop that housed the engine to supply electricity for the radio.

The buildings were connected by a series of underground snow tunnels to keep the men out of the fierce blizzards and eliminate the possibility of them getting lost. The upper walls of the snow

The boxes of food were stacked up and would be covered in snow, forming underground tunnels.

tunnels were lined with wooden crates of food and supplies. They were very dark and narrow, barely wide enough for two people to walk side by side.

One snow tunnel in particular captured Igloo's interest — it was the one called Dog Town. Inside this tunnel there were niches carved out of the sides of the wall for the sled dogs' crates. The dogs were leashed inside and spaced far enough apart so they couldn't fight with one another.

Byrd told Igloo to stay out of Dog Town, which was good advice. But Igloo didn't plan to take it.

SEVEN

DARK NIGHTS

MARCH 1929, ANTARCTICA

Each morning, at the sound of reveille, Igloo would wake up in his cozy bed. It was situated at the foot of Byrd's bunk bed in the Administration Building. Igloo's friend, carpenter Chips Gould, had made it especially for him. Chips had lined the inside of it with soft wool shearling, and every night, before Igloo went to sleep, Byrd would cover him up in a warm blanket.

Igloo was usually an early riser, but some mornings, when the temperature in the room was below zero, it was hard for Igloo to leave the warmth of his blanket. But he didn't want to miss breakfast. On those days, he would wait until the last minute before jumping out of his bed to accompany Byrd to the Mess Hall.

Despite the chill in his bones, Igloo always made a point of saying good morning to everyone with a wag of his tail or by leaning into their legs as he walked by. Sometimes it was while the men were busy getting dressed in their warm clothes. Other times, it was before they took their seats at the dining room table.

In the Mess Hall, Igloo and Byrd were greeted with the aroma of coffee wafting in the air. Cook Tennant always kept a pot of fresh coffee brewing from breakfast time until ten o'clock at night.

"Melted snow was poor drinking," said Tennant. "So some of them drank as many as thirty cups a day of my coffee; and they seemed to think it was as good as they could want at home."

Byrd preferred either hot tea with two lumps of sugar and cream, or hot chocolate. Igloo preferred none. But as soon as everyone was served breakfast, Igloo made his rounds, walking to each person to see what treats they would share with him from their plates.

Usually, everyone started with a bowl of hot

Igloo takes his rightful place at the head of the table with Byrd.

cereal with powdered milk. Igloo looked forward to the times when Cook Tennant made bacon — it was his favorite. Sometimes Cook made fried eggs for breakfast. It was so cold the eggs were frozen in their shells, and he had to boil them first before he could fry them. And on occasion he made chicken à la king on toast. Cook Tennant also learned how to cook whale, penguin, and seal meat.

"Whale meat is good, tastes like a tender steak if you get a young one. Older ones taste fishy," said

Tennant. "We caught a young ninety-ton whale. You carefully trim all the fat layers off the back of the whale and then get down to the steak meat. With the penguins and seals I would soak the meat in salt and vinegar water for hours and then roast or boil it. Great eating, too, I tell you."

After breakfast, everyone had a lot of work to do. Along with the pilots, mechanics, cooks, and dogsled drivers, there was a team of scientists. At the time, not much was known about Antarctica, especially where Little America was situated. Although the highlight of the expedition was to see if Byrd could fly a plane to the South Pole and back, it was also a scientific expedition. The primary interest was in mapping the unknown continent and determining if it had any natural resources, such as coal.

Some of the scientists in Little America were old friends of Igloo. He had met them on his trip to the Arctic. Cyclone Haines was on the expedition studying the weather, and Malcolm Hanson was in charge of the radio.

But some were new to Igloo. Paul Siple, a twenty-one-year-old college student, Eagle Scout, and an assistant Scout master, was chosen out of thousands of Boy Scouts applicants to accompany Byrd to the Antarctic. Siple was studying the biology of penguins and seals.

The chief scientist on the expedition, and the second in command to Byrd, was the good-natured Larry Gould (who was not related to Chips Gould). Gould was a professor of geology, and he was there to study the glaciers and rocks.

Shortly after arriving in the Antarctic, Byrd had given his airplanes a test run in the cold weather and began surveying and mapping the Antarctic. Aerial photographer, Captain Ashley McKinley, who had the rare distinction of being a pilot in all three classes of aircraft — balloons, dirigibles, and airplanes — brought his fifty-pound camera on board and took photos out the window. On Byrd's first flight, the Rockefeller Mountains were discovered. Byrd named them after John D. Rockefeller, Jr., because from the beginning he had always had faith in Byrd and helped fund Byrd's expedition.

Professor Gould couldn't wait to examine the rocks from the Rockefeller Mountains, especially since no one had ever seen them before. The rocks could unearth secrets about the Antarctic, such as whether any plants or animals had ever lived there.

So in early March, when it was the beginning of fall in Antarctica, Professor Gould asked if he could take a team to Rockefeller Mountains, 125 miles east of Little America, to do some geological work. Byrd was reluctant to let them go.

"Poor Larry," Byrd wrote in his diary. "He has been compelled to dull his geological hammer on the ends of boxes while the rocks in the Rockefellers fairly cried out for investigation. Such a journey would be very important, but, frankly I am not eager to see him undertake it at this advanced period with winter so near. The weather has been stormy and cold, and I am not sure the flight can be made without considerable risk."

But every morning Professor Gould would look at the sky and ask Cyclone Haines about the weather report. The outlook was always stormy, and Gould would rib Cyclone about his lack of skills in controlling the weather. Still, Gould was hopeful, and every day he would pack some equipment while waiting for a good weather report.

It finally came. Cyclone said there were good weather conditions for flying, and Byrd agreed to let Gould go. Bernt Balchen, who piloted Byrd's transatlantic flight, was piloting the single-engine Fokker plane, and the square-headed Harold June, whose blue eyes twinkled whenever he laughed — which was often — was operating the radio.

With his bags already packed with his two prized geology hammers, Gould had a big smile on his face as he carried them to the plane. When Byrd watched their plane take flight, he had misgivings, until he received his first radio message from Gould.

"Everything fine with plane about forty miles from base headed towards Mts.," the message read.

At dinnertime, Byrd received another message that they had landed safely. He was relieved for the time being. That is, until a week later. That's when Byrd stopped hearing from them altogether. Every hour Malcolm Hanson tried to radio Gould. There was no reply. A terrible thought crept into everyone's mind — the plane had crashed and Gould, Balchen, and June were dead.

"I should never have let them go," said Byrd. "I knew I shouldn't at this time of year, but it seemed necessary. I shall never forgive myself if anything happens to him."

Igloo stuck close by, sitting on Byrd's lap, while Byrd tried to figure out how to send a rescue team for them without getting anyone killed in the process. Treacherous weather plagued Little America, making a rescue by plane or dogsled nearly impossible. Making matters worse, Byrd wasn't sure of their exact location since Larry hadn't radioed in to tell them.

As each day passed, blizzards dumped snow on Little America, reminding them that the long, dark winter nights were quickly approaching. For the next several days, Byrd continued to ask Cyclone for the weather report. Finally, on March 19, five days after they lost contact with Gould, Cyclone predicted better weather.

"Frankly, I consider a takeoff dangerous," said Cyclone. "But it may be the best chance you will have . . . about one chance in three, I should say, that you will find good weather all the way. . . . You can't tell what this weather will do, anyway."

Byrd figured as long as there was a chance, no matter how slim, he would take it because it might be his only chance for a rescue. They warmed the motors of the Fairchild airplane, and Dean Smith, an airmail pilot who had plenty of experience flying in bad weather, was at the controls. Byrd would navigate and Malcolm Hanson would operate the radio.

The plane took off down a bumpy, snowy runway. It finally lifted off and headed toward the Rockefeller Mountains.

After Byrd left, Igloo was inconsolable. And just when he thought his troubles could not get any worse, they did. When Igloo went into his room, he found Holly, a grouchy sled dog with a quick temper, lying down on his specially made bed. And to top it off, she was there with six new puppies.

Igloo was furious. But Holly glared at him and bared her fangs. Igloo promptly ran out of his room. He was so distraught that he wandered aimlessly through Little America, trying to collect himself. Finally, he ran for help. He alerted Cook Tennant and Captain McKinley, barking and nipping at their pant legs, trying to get them to come take a look.

Captain McKinley followed Igloo to his room, and he immediately understood Igloo's dilemma. McKinley very carefully persuaded Holly to leave Igloo's bed and return to her kennel with her pups. After much coaxing, she finally complied, moving out of Igloo's bed, at least for now. She wasn't about to let Igloo have the final say on the matter.

In the meantime, the rescue plane had returned. But Byrd wasn't on it. Neither was Larry Gould nor Malcolm Hanson. They were forced to stay behind because the load was too heavy for the plane. But Dean Smith, Bernt Balchen, and Harold June were safely back, and everyone wanted to know what had happened.

Soon after Gould, Balchen, and June had reached the foot of the Rockefeller Mountains, they had tied down their plane and set up a tent. At first, the weather was calm, allowing Gould to collect some rock specimens, but then the wind started to pick up.

"The next morning the tent was flapping in the wind, the sides snapping like reports in a gun," said June. "There was a tiny hole near the head of my sleeping bag and I peeked out at the plane. . . . I rubbed my eyes and looked again. I'm darned if the propeller wasn't turning over despite the cold which must have made the oil stiff."

They quickly got out of their sleeping bags and ran to the plane, trying desperately for hours to anchor it.

"Larry [Gould] and I were holding the left wing down with lines . . . while Bernt dug snow blocks and piled them," said June.

But it was futile. It was soon a hurricane force wind, and they ran to their tent to take cover while the wind ripped the plane apart.

"How it blew," said June. "I never heard such a sound. When it stopped it was so quiet that it hurt. It will linger a long time in my memory. I can hear that wind and feel the flying blocks of snow hit me yet."

After the storm wrecked their plane, the weather improved somewhat, with temperatures reaching a high of thirty-two degrees above zero. It was difficult for them to sit and wait, but they were concerned if they tried to walk back, no one would ever find them on the vast snowy desert. On the day when they finally heard the rescue plane, they grabbed some smoke bombs and ignited them.

In the rescue plane overhead, Smith tapped Byrd's arm and pointed out the window. Byrd could see a column of smoke and a flash of light.

"The first thought that came to my head was: Thank God, at least one of them is alive," said Byrd.

Balchen and June had placed flags on the snow to indicate where Smith should land the plane. It wasn't easy. The terrain was rough, and they landed with a thud and a bounce. When Byrd got out of the plane, he carried his sleeping bag to one side, knelt down, and prayed. He thanked God that everyone was alive.

"I knew he would come when it was possible," said Gould. "He did not say a word about the loss of the plane. No one who has not experienced it can appreciate his sense of fairness and justice, his magnanimous and generous consideration for others."

Back at Little America bad weather had again delayed a second flight to the Rockefeller Mountains to pick up Byrd, Gould, and Hanson. It was an anxious time for Igloo. If a plane couldn't fly to pick Byrd up, then he and the others would have to walk back to Little America, and that would take at least three weeks — if they made it back at all. And to top it off, Holly kept making her way back into Igloo's room, trying to commandeer his bed for her puppies.

It was two more days of worry for Igloo before the weather cleared and Byrd made it back to

Little America. The night Byrd finally returned, he found Igloo sleeping fitfully in his specially made bed, with his nose over the side of his box and a look of utter disgust on his face. Igloo couldn't stand the lingering scent of Holly. And Holly was relentless, coming back into Igloo's bed with her puppies whenever the opportunity presented itself, which was more often than Igloo could bear to think about.

With Byrd back, he was able to remedy Igloo's problem. Each time Holly came into the room, Byrd always took her and her pups back to her kennel. He finally moved Holly's kennel next to the door of the Administration Building, which she eventually accepted as her new home. In the end, the rescue mission had been a close call for everyone at Little America — dogs and humans alike.

Just when Igloo thought he'd made himself clear on the subject — no dogs allowed in the Administration Building except him — Spy arrived. It happened early one morning when the temperature was forty below zero: so cold a person can hear the crackling sound of his breath freezing. Byrd found Spy shivering in his crate in Dog Town and nearly dead from the cold. The hard work of hauling the heavy sled had taken a toll on him. Spy was so cold he could barely walk, and one of his paws was so sore and lame, he dragged it across the ground.

Byrd brought the friendly lead dog into the Administration Building, and Spy — with his eyes half-closed — sat down stiffly by the warm stove. He let out a mournful groan from the pain.

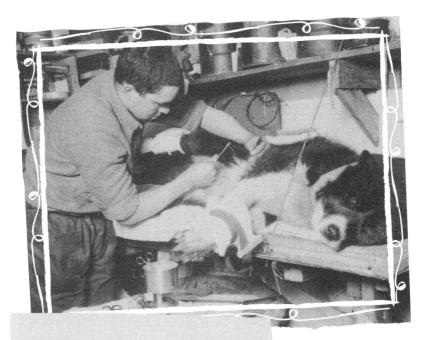

The dog hospital in Little America.

Spy's dog driver, Norman Vaughan, who loved Spy, was worried that Spy was in too much pain and should be put down.

"Let's give him a chance," said Byrd. "He has earned it and perhaps he can have a few comfortable months more."

Byrd placed some canvas bags in a corner of his room, far away from Igloo's bed. Even so, Igloo was furious about this new arrangement, and he barked unhappily at Spy.

"The only available space in the camp at the time was in my room," said Byrd. "And old Spy lay there for two days, much to the disgust of Igloo who attacked him whenever my back was turned."

When Spy gained some strength and started to hold out his paw to be shaken, Byrd took him outside for a walk, hoping the exercise would help. Spy spotted his brothers, Moody and Watch, hooked to a sled and limped over to see them. Moody and Watch were lying down with their legs stretched out on the snow. Spy sat down between them. His brothers licked his face and his sore paw. Watch gently pushed his head into Spy's while all three cuddled, keeping Spy warm.

Then the dog driver cracked his whip and yelled

"Yake!" for straight ahead. The dogs stood up and took off running. Spy gathered all of his strength and ran as fast as he could, running alongside the team and trying to find his place as their lead.

"It was one of the most beautiful things I have ever seen, and for a penny I would pluck a moral from it," said Byrd. "The whole camp stopped working at the sight, and watched with wonder how Moody and Watch nuzzled the veteran, and laid their paws on him in a most extraordinary gesture. That these wild and untrammeled animals should be capable of harboring so deep and lasting sentiment was beyond understanding."

Igloo, on the other hand, had reached his boiling point with Spy. In a show of appreciation to Byrd, Spy tried to climb up onto his lap. Igloo wasn't about to let that happen, and with all of his strength, Igloo heaved Spy from Byrd's lap.

Spy didn't fight back. Instead, he gave Igloo a hangdog look and walked out of the Administration Building, never to return. Spy went back to his brothers in Dog Town — where, as far as Igloo was concerned, he belonged.

Although Spy never worked as a sled dog again, he recovered. And every time Igloo would see him, Igloo had the decency to act contrite. But Spy didn't hold it against him.

On April 17, 1929, the sun disappeared and darkness fell on Little America for the next four months. Below ground, dim lights glowed inside Little America, and Byrd's expedition was faced with the challenge of keeping busy while being cooped up.

Byrd was usually sitting at his desk, chewing on the tip of his pencil, and working out the problems with flying in the Antarctic. The main one was figuring out how to carry four men plus all of the food, fuel, and equipment — especially when they flew over the enormous mountains. He had to consider all possibilities and make contingency plans if they crashed.

As Byrd worked, Igloo was faced with the challenge of keeping warm. Like the sled dogs, Igloo grew a thicker coat of fur. He even had an extra clump on the end of his tail, making it look like a toothbrush. There were stoves to warm the rooms, but heat rises, and there was a fifty-degree difference between the temperature at the floor of the rooms in Little America and at the ceiling.

Igloo and Byrd planning the flight over the South Pole.

Ice formed on the floor, and everyone's feet were cold, especially Igloo's. To keep their feet and legs warm, the men wore their fur pants and boots. Igloo learned to lift his paws up one after the other, as if he were walking on hot coals, to try to keep them warm.

Despite the cold and darkness, Byrd and Igloo continued their daily walks outside. But during the walks, Igloo would sometimes suddenly lie down. He would hold up a paw and cry out, refusing to budge until Byrd picked him up and rubbed his frozen paw. Once it was warmed up, Igloo would jump down and continue walking. That is, until his paw got cold again.

When the temperature dipped to thirty degrees below zero, it was just too cold for Igloo outdoors. Even though it was one of his most favorite things to do, Igloo just couldn't bring himself to go outside, especially if the wind was blowing.

Instead, Igloo preferred to play with his new favorite toy — the rubber ball that squeaked like

Byrd and Igloo exploring the ice in Antarctica.

a cat. For Igloo, the trick was to find someone to play ball with him. Byrd played at least three times a day, by hiding it in various spots around the Administration Building so Igloo could look gleefully around for it. But sometimes Byrd was too busy.

During those times, Igloo would glance stealthily around to see if anyone happened to notice the ball. If no one reached for it, Igloo would push it with his nose, rolling it toward anyone nearby. As someone reached for it, Igloo would pounce on the ball, making it squeak, and he would let out a growl before dashing off, wagging his tail happily. But if no one was willing to play, Igloo squeaked it continually until someone finally grabbed it — sometimes just to stop the noise.

On occasion Cook Tennant gave Igloo a bone, and Igloo would set to work finding the perfect place to bury it. Since the ground was frozen, he had to find alternative places to hide his treasure. Sometimes Igloo would bury it under his bed or under a rug. But one of the best spots he found was hiding it at the bottom of Byrd's sleeping bag.

Nevertheless, on the days when Igloo tired of these games or when everyone was too busy, he sometimes played with the pack of twenty wild sled dog puppies — new friends that Igloo tolerated and usually ran into on his way to the Mess Hall.

"Literally, they ran wild," said Byrd. "They could not be captured, but prowled the camp, feeding on scraps of food that were put out for them, enduring the lowest temperatures without visible discomfort."

Igloo was always looking for a way to sneak inside Dog Town. The tunnel was dark — with the exception of the dogs' glowing eyes — and it echoed with barks and howls, and had a pungent smell of dogs and raw seal meat.

A run through Dog Town was always a death-defying experience — even for the men. One time when Chips Gould went there to repair a gate, one of the pups ran off with his lantern. In the darkness, Gould got lost and he feared a run-in with Oulie, the meanest dog in Dog Town. Luckily, Gould ran into Birch, one of the sweetest dogs. Birch guided Gould safely out of the dark tunnel and to the Mess Hall, where Gould gave Birch a whole leg of lamb in appreciation.

Igloo knew that if he ran through Dog Town, he had to be quick, timing it just right so the dogs, who were chained, couldn't catch him. When Igloo streaked by, total chaos followed, with the dogs trying to bite and slash him with their claws. A run through Dog Town usually ended with Igloo lying on the table in the Mess Hall with his good friend, Doc Coman, patching him up with stitches. Even so, this never stopped Igloo. Like Byrd, it was the danger that thrilled him.

Two of Igloo's good friends. Cook Tennant (on the left) who Igloo could rely on for a good bite, and Dr. Coman (on the right) who Igloo could rely on to patch him up after a run through Dog Town.

"He had long since got over the shock they first gave him during the trip South on the *City of New York*. He feared not even the biggest dog among them," said Byrd. "No doubt, he believed he was a great fighter because we saved his life so often. He was even condescending in his attitude, especially toward the pups, although his life was really in great danger. We had to watch him very carefully, because when he was allowed to run loose he invariably made for Dog Town. Almost always he returned in need of medical attention."

One day a terrible noise was coming from Dog Town. It sounded like a dog was dying — yelping and crying for help. The men realized the cries were coming from Igloo, and they were worried that he was half-dead from a fight.

Someone ran into the darkened tunnel with a lantern and in the shadows found Igloo sitting down with a paw outstretched. Uninjured, Igloo was in pain from the cold. He was howling for someone — preferably Byrd — to warm his paws.

When Byrd heard the news, he did one better for Igloo. Byrd consulted Martin Ronne, who fired up his sewing machine and made Igloo his very own snowsuit and boots. The parka and pants

Inside Dog Town. Igloo was instructed to stay out, which he gleefully ignored.

were made of camel's-hair wool, and the boots, which laced up, were lined with wool and stuffed with senna grass to keep his feet dry.

Igloo looked adorable in his new snowsuit and boots. And the men sitting around the table laughed with delight. Igloo, on the other hand, was absolutely humiliated by the idea of wearing a snowsuit and boots. He sat frozen on the table, unwilling to move.

"Come, come, Igloo!" said Byrd. "You can't feel quite that bad. Walk around a bit. It's really a perfect fit."

Byrd gave Igloo a reassuring nudge, and Igloo walked stiff legged around the table, receiving pats of encouragement from Byrd and the men. Igloo wagged his tail hesitantly.

The snowsuit and boots kept Igloo warm and snug, but Igloo soon found out that the snowsuit and boots also made him a walking target. The first time the pups saw Igloo in his new snowsuit and boots, they could barely contain themselves.

Igloo in his custom-designed parka and snow boots.

They were falling all over one another as each one tried to reach Igloo first. Immediately, they sunk their razor-sharp teeth into Igloo's parka and yanked him in all directions.

Needless to say, Igloo was hopping mad. At first he tried to control his temper. Igloo never liked to look childish in front of Byrd. But when the pups ripped holes in his new warm coat, Igloo wasn't going to stand for it.

He turned around and faced the pack of pups. With his brown ears flat against his head, Igloo charged toward them, striking them like a bowling ball against the pins. The puppies rolled and were stunned — most of them took off running. But a few remained, and Igloo took them on in a dogfight. Byrd quickly broke it up.

Igloo continued his walk with Byrd. The pups walked behind them, keeping a safe distance from Igloo, who was still fuming because his parka now looked ragged — its epaulets were torn and there was a large hole in the back.

But Ronne fixed the snowsuit for Igloo. He sewed some patches on the parka, and it was almost as good as new. The pups never dared to rip it again, and Igloo learned to like his snowsuit

Igloo and Byrd surrounded by the sled-dog puppies.

and boots. Whenever he wanted to go for a walk with Byrd, he would grab his snowsuit and drop it at Byrd's feet.

The darkness that fell on Little America finally lifted on August 22, 1929, when the sun returned, peeking over the horizon. To mark the occasion, the expedition raised the American flag and played a bugle call on the Victrola. It was time to dig out from the harsh winter and make the final preparations for Byrd's riskiest flight yet — to the South Pole and back.

Portrait of Byrd and Igloo by artist Richard Adam.

EIGHT

FLYING THE IMPOSSIBLE

Although spring was in the air, it was still bitterly cold in Antarctica. Fierce blizzards still plagued Little America, and the temperatures still dropped to sixty-eight degrees below zero. Even so, it was a busy time gearing up for the flight over the South Pole, which would take months of preparations.

"Everyone is at work at something — sewing parkas and socks, repairing harnesses, testing tents, relashing sledges," Byrd wrote in his diary.

Professor Larry Gould and his geological party were planning their scientific expedition. They would be gone for three months and travel some 1,500 miles. Gould and his team were going to map and study the mountains and leave emergency food and fuel caches along the flight route for Byrd. The Supporting Party would leave beforehand to break the trail for the Geological Party. Both parties were using dogsleds. But preparing the sled dogs was proving to be more difficult than anyone expected.

"We have had a wild time with the dogs," said Byrd. "They are so overjoyed to be aboveground once more that they have forgotten all manners and training, and run about the camp like lunatics."

Boy Scout Paul Siple was tasked with capturing the unruly, wild pups and teaching them to pull a sled. On October 15, the day the Geological Party was leaving for a two-day preliminary test, Byrd and Igloo were there to see them off. Siple offered to take Byrd and Igloo on for the first several miles of the expedition.

"He gave me what I would conservatively describe as the wildest ride I ever had," said Byrd.

With Holly as the lead dog and the pack of wild pups harnessed behind her, Holly took off running. The sled zoomed across the bay ice

Igloo inspects the equipment.

as if it were on fire. Very quickly, the pups got tangled in the harness, and the sled suddenly overturned.

While Byrd and Siple tried to straighten out the lines, Holly refused to stand still, making their job even more difficult. Finally, they took off again. But the pups once again got tangled. As Byrd started to get off the sled, Holly suddenly jerked forward. The supplies flew off the sled — along with Byrd and Igloo — while Holly and the pups took off sprinting, not stopping for the next half mile.

"I was fond of Holly," said Byrd. "But she was mightily in wrong for the moment."

After that, the pups and Holly were on their very best behavior and did a good job, even overtaking some of the bigger teams of sled dogs. After two hours, Byrd and Igloo bade farewell to the Geological Party. They watched the other dogsled teams run up the slope and disappear behind it, only to see them go up another slope, then disappear again.

When the dogs and sleds were no longer in their line of sight, Byrd and Igloo returned to their sled only to find that the pups had chewed up their harnesses and were once again running wild. Byrd and Igloo hitched a ride on a different sled back to Little America.

Two weeks later, Byrd's Ford airplane, the *Floyd Bennett*, was taken out of its ice hangar, a ten-foot hole with walls made from blocks of rock-hard snow and ice. It was covered over with a tarp and drifted snow. Byrd's crew shoveled away the snow and sliced away the walls. The plane was

Igloo and Byrd unpacking crates and assembling the plane in Antarctica.

in good shape, having survived the treacherous weather, but it needed some work before it would be ready to fly.

The plane was in pieces and had to be reassembled. The wings were wet and had to be dried using blowtorches before being reattached, the fuel lines needed to be cleaned out, and the mechanics worked on the three engines, making sure everything was just right.

Igloo took his job of supporting Byrd very seriously, and he always stuck close by. He didn't want to be left behind when Byrd took flight for the South Pole. To make sure this didn't happen, Igloo had a plan.

In the meantime, Byrd was waiting for a good weather report. Sunshine was absolutely essential for a successful flight.

"Flying down here with a cloud-covered sky is like flying in a world that has turned to milk," said Byrd. "There is nothing to check on. Horizons disappear and there is no way to tell where the snow begins, how rough the surface is, nor even how high we are above it. . . . When the course goes over mountains whose peaks tower higher than the plane can fly, good visibility is required to get between the peaks over the glaciers."

Finally, on Thanksgiving Day, November 28, 1929, Cyclone Haines predicted good weather. It was time for Byrd to take flight.

The plane was loaded with sleeping bags, fuel, oil, tents, clothing, sacks of food, a small sled, stoves, and photographic equipment. Each item was carefully weighed to make sure the plane did not exceed 15,000 pounds. If the plane was too heavy, it wouldn't be able to fly over the mountains.

"For many months our minds had been concentrated on the knotty problem of getting over this rampart. . . . We made very careful tests with the plane and had checked and rechecked our figures for weeks . . . there must be no mistake about our load," said Byrd. "Every ounce of food, every piece of clothing, everything that went into that plane, including ourselves, had to be weighed carefully."

The last thing Byrd put on the plane was an American flag weighted with a stone from Floyd Bennett's grave. Byrd was going to drop it on the South Pole.

"It had been the three of us — Bennett, Balchen, and myself — who had set out on this job two years ago, and the three of us would be together at the finish, for we knew that Floyd Bennett's spirit flew with us," said Byrd. "He had selected the Ford plane, prepared it and flown it, and had helped with our early plans, so that his genius and his friendship were with us helping us to reach our goal."

Dressed in their polar fur suits, Byrd, Balchen, Harold June, and Ashley McKinley were ready to attempt the first flight over the South Pole.

Byrd in the library before his South Pole flight. He's holding the American flag and stone that he planned to drop over the South Pole.

Before taking off, Byrd made a final, last-minute check of the airplane. When he reached the back of the plane, he was surprised to discover Igloo comfortably settled in and ready to go.

Igloo was greatly disappointed when Byrd removed him from the plane. His cunning plan to be a stowaway was foiled.

"Igloo didn't go along in the plane. . . . That wouldn't have been right," said Byrd. "In case of an accident what would happen to a dog?"

From the snowy runway, Igloo stood among the men and watched the plane disappear over the horizon. Inside the plane, Balchen was busy at the controls while June listened intently to the roar of the motors. He was monitoring the plane's fuel consumption, making sure they didn't run out. Throughout the flight, McKinley never stopped snapping photos. He was creating an aerial map of their flight, the first of its kind, and it was of great geographical value.

Byrd was all over the plane, shifting his position so he could take observations to navigate, maintaining their course with his dependable sun compass and drift indicator. It wasn't easy to move around in the plane. There were piles of supplies smack in the middle of the fuselage. The smell from the gasoline fumes and the rarefied air made it hard to breathe. And there was a cold wind that blew through the plane, making them glad they were wearing their furs. Even so, for the first few hours, they were able to enjoy the scenery as they headed toward the Queen Maud Range.

"Flying over this mysterious Barrier never loses its fascination . . . Great white glaciers flowed into the Barrier . . . alpine snow-covered peaks towering high over the Barrier that glistened like fire from the sun's reflection so that they looked like great volcanoes in eruption," said Byrd.

But soon the perilous mountain peaks were directly ahead of them, and just beyond, on the 10,000-foot plateau, was the South Pole. Byrd had a do-or-die decision to make — which route to take — flying over Axel Heiberg Glacier or Liv Glacier.

They both looked dangerous — with their narrow passes sandwiched between gigantic peaks. If the plane was too heavy, they would crash right into the mountains.

"I was by no means certain which glacier I should choose for the ascent," said Byrd.

Byrd went forward and stood behind Balchen. He looked out the window and studied the peaks. Byrd knew that the Axel Heiberg Glacier was 10,500-feet high. But he didn't know if the pass between the peaks was too narrow. If they were too narrow, the air currents could push the heavily loaded plane to the ground.

And nothing was known about Liv Glacier. From where Byrd was standing, the pass looked wide enough. But he couldn't see if there were mountains behind it. And if there were mountains, he didn't know if they would be able to fly over them.

"Doubtless, a flip of the coin would have served us well," said Byrd.

Byrd chose Liv Glacier. The pass looked wider than and not as high as Axel Heiberg Glacier. Still, it was a gamble.

"Once we entered the pass," said Byrd, "there would be no retreat. It offered no room for turn. If power was lost momentarily or if the air became excessively rough, we could only go ahead, or down. We had to climb, and there was only one way in which we could climb."

Balchen flew the plane toward Liv Glacier and approached it with caution and confidence. The plane's wings shook from the changing air pressure, and they hit a patch of turbulence. The violence of the turbulence forced Balchen to turn the plane slightly to the left, and soon they were caught in heavy downdrafts.

As the plane approached the glacier's peak,

the plane was too low — it was carrying too much weight. They were going to crash.

Balchen was gesturing wildly, trying to be heard over the roar of the engines.

"Overboard! Overboard!"

June stood with his hand on the dump valve of the main fuel tank. If he pulled it, six hundred gallons of gasoline would be unloaded. Byrd gestured to wait. He had to decide — food or fuel?

"If gasoline, I thought, we might as well stop there and turn back," said Byrd. "We could never get back to the base from the Pole. If food, the lives of all us would be jeopardized in the event of a forced landing."

It only took a moment for Byrd to decide. McKinley had already moved one of the 125-pound bags of food to the trap door. One bag was one month's supply of food for four men.

"A bag of food overboard," Byrd yelled to June.

McKinley was standing by the trapdoor, and June signaled to throw it out.

"Shall I do it, Commander?" McKinley asked Byrd.

Byrd nodded his head. They watched the brown bag fall, spinning to the ground. The plane started to gain altitude. Balchen looked back and smiled. He moved the plane to the right, and flew over the lowest part of the pass.

But, once again, the plane hit turbulence, knocking them around "like a cork in a washtub." They could barely stay on their feet. Very slowly, the plane inched up. Even so, the wheel suddenly turned loosely in Balchen's hand.

"Quick! Dump more!" Balchen shouted over the din of the engines.

Byrd pointed to a bag of food. McKinley opened the trap door, the freezing air burning his face, and he dumped another bag. It was their last chance.

"We could not let any more food go," said Byrd. "Nor could we dump gasoline and have any reserve supply left for reaching the Pole. There was nothing more to dump. We must make it."

They watched the bag of food shatter soundlessly against the glacier below them. Suddenly, the plane lifted higher into the air. And when they reached the towering pass, they flew over it with about three hundred feet to spare. The usually quiet Balchen let out a shout of joy.

After ten hours of flying, at 1:14 a.m., Byrd

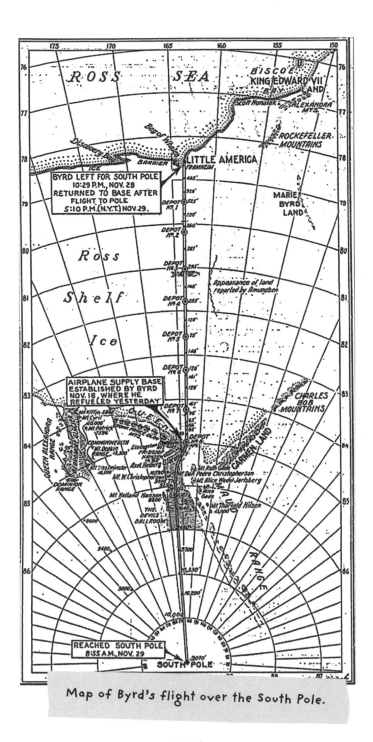

Map of Byrd's flight over the South Pole.

passed a note to June. It read, "My calculations indicate we have reached the vicinity of the South Pole. Flying high for survey. Soon turn north."

Byrd opened the trapdoor and dropped the American flag and a piece of stone from Floyd Bennett's grave. Byrd stood and they "saluted the spirit of our gallant comrade and our country's flag."

When June radioed the news to Little America from the plane, everyone cheered. Igloo joined in by hopping up onto the Mess Hall table and barking with all his might. And nine hours later, Igloo was the first to hear the hum of the airplane on its return. He stood on the runway, running back and forth excitedly as the plane landed. The men tossed their hats in the air and cheered. And Igloo was one of the first to greet Byrd when he got off the plane, running alongside him, jumping up, and patting Byrd's leg.

Everyone hurried into the Mess Hall to have some hot drinks from Cook Tennant's galley. There was a lot to celebrate on Byrd and Igloo's Antarctic adventure. And they would soon find out that the celebration was just beginning.

GLORY DAYS

NINE

JUNE 20, 1930: WASHINGTON, DC

It was a hot and sunny day when Igloo found himself on the White House Lawn. He was just a half mile away from the candy store where Maris Boggs found him on that rainy day in January four and a half years ago.

But today, Igloo was attending a reception in honor of Byrd and his team, of which Igloo was a vital part. President Hoover, who became the president in 1929, had a passion for geology, and he was presenting Byrd with a medal for "the first attainment of the geographical South Pole and for distinguished contributions to world knowledge

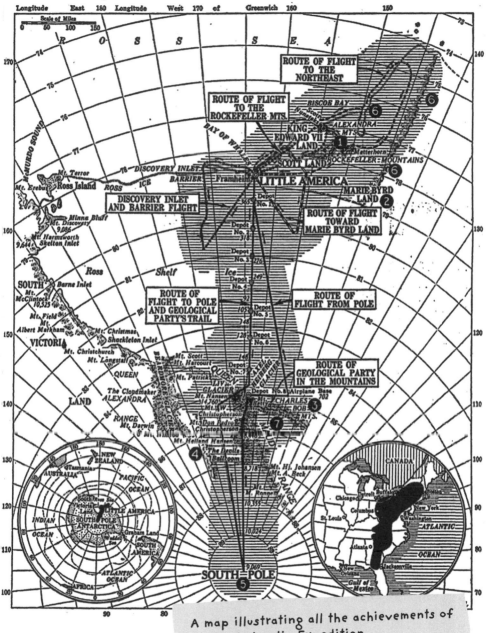

A map illustrating all the achievements of Byrd's Antarctic Expedition.

of Antarctica." Byrd was also promoted to the rank of admiral. When Igloo met the president, he received a pat on the head.

"Great explorers . . . do not merely add to the sum of human knowledge," said President Hoover. "But also they add immensely to the sum of human inspiration."

A few days later, Igloo received a gold medal, too. The Tail Waggers' Club, a humanitarian organization that only had dogs as members and strived "to make the lot of the dog a better one in this world," presented one to Igloo for services rendered on the Antarctic expedition.

Since Byrd and Igloo had arrived back from the Antarctic, it had been a whirlwind of parades and receptions. It started with a ticker-tape parade in New York, followed by a midnight train ride to Washington, DC.

A few days after meeting the President, Byrd and Igloo went to their hometown of Boston for another ticker-tape parade to welcome them home. As soon as they got off the train, pandemonium broke out. Thousands of people crowded around them, trying to catch a glimpse. Soldiers, sailors, and the National Guard were

The ticker-tape parade for Byrd in Boston.

needed to give Byrd and Igloo a military escort.

During the parade, the sun was shining brightly. Thirty airplanes flew overhead and there was a thirteen-gun salute. Sitting in the backseat of a convertible car, Byrd's gold epaulets sparkled on his white uniform. As the car drove slowly down the streets of Boston, Byrd smiled and waved to the cheering crowds lining the sidewalks. Igloo sat with an air of importance on top of the back seat. He could hear the crowds shouting, "There's Igloo!"

Igloo riding in the car during a parade.

Later in the afternoon, they arrived at their home on 9 Brimmer Street. After receiving hugs and kisses from the family, Igloo made his way upstairs to the playroom. Inside a toy chest, he found his beloved toy goat. He clutched it in his mouth. Home sweet home.

After a summer family vacation in New Hampshire — where Igloo got sprayed by a skunk and pierced by a porcupine — Byrd and Igloo set off on a lecture tour.

Byrd was in demand. Everyone wanted to hear about his trip to the Antarctic. He gave lectures in nearly every state. And Igloo faithfully attended Byrd's lectures. When the audience applauded, Igloo joined in and barked his appreciation.

Byrd and Igloo celebrating their return in Boston.

When Byrd went to the numerous luncheons and banquets, Igloo went, too. Sometimes Igloo felt shy and hid under the table. But he could always be lured out to say hello if there was a sweet treat, especially cake.

Wherever Byrd went, Igloo went, too — even if he wasn't invited. Igloo wouldn't have wanted it any other way. He was, after all, Byrd's best friend.

Byrd & Igloo: best friends.

EPILOGUE

On Monday evening, April 20, 1931, Byrd received word from home that Igloo, who was taking a break from the tour, was very, very ill. For the last several days, Igloo had been suffering from severe indigestion. Although three veterinarians had examined him, Igloo was not getting better.

Byrd immediately cancelled all of the lectures he was scheduled to give that week and he hopped on the next train to Boston, rushing to be by Igloo's side.

But Byrd was too late. Igloo died before he made it home.

The nation mourned for Igloo, and Byrd

A portrait of Igloo in all his glory.

received thousands of condolence letters. One even offered him another dog. Byrd politely declined.

"Igloo cannot be replaced," said Byrd. "Those of you who are dogs' friends know that a dog can be, and usually is, a better friend to his master than he is to himself."

Heartbroken, Byrd held a funeral for Igloo. With his hat in his hand, Byrd watched the white coffin with silver handles lowered into the grave. Byrd's son, Dickie, walked over and dropped a bouquet of sweet peas on the coffin. When Igloo's grave was covered over with dirt, Byrd carefully placed a bouquet of white roses on it.

"He taught me much," said Byrd. "Igloo . . . opened my eyes to the facts that animals can think and suffer, be loyal and gallant. . . . He was my good companion for five years and, as the stone over his grave testifies, 'He Was More Than a Friend.'"

Byrd placing a bouquet of white roses on Igloo's grave.

AUTHOR'S NOTE

From the moment Byrd and Bennett landed their plane on the icy runway in Spitsbergen on May 9, 1926, their claim of being the first to fly over the North Pole has been debated — with no end in sight.

The Italian and Norwegian newspaper reporters who were there to cover Amundsen's flight over the North Pole were the first to question Byrd's claim. It's no wonder. During the time that Byrd was an explorer, there was a lot at stake. Explorers were celebrated, larger-than-life superheroes, and whoever was the *first* to get there was assured fame and fortune.

As soon as Byrd returned from the Arctic, he sent his navigational records to the U.S. Navy and the National Geographic Society for verification. After carefully examining his report, they agreed that Byrd had reached the North Pole. To this day, they have never wavered in their decision.

But for those who doubted Byrd's claim, questions, theories, and rumors simmered over the years. Could the *Josephine Ford* have flown that fast? Did they really try to fly to the North Pole?

In 1996, seventy years after Byrd and Bennett's

historic flight, Byrd's long-lost personal diary was found among all of his boxes and bags of records, papers, writings, and artifacts. Byrd was a meticulous record keeper, and he kept everything — even Igloo's parka and boots.

Inside the diary were his handwritten notes to Bennett during their flight to the North Pole. One message indicates that there were strong, intermittent winds during their flight, which, if tailwinds, would have allowed the airplane to fly faster. And Byrd continuously updated Bennett about their distance from the North Pole up until his last message indicating that they had, in fact, reached the North Pole.

Byrd's diary is archived at the Byrd Polar Research Center at the Ohio State University in Columbus, Ohio. And it can be requested along with Igloo's parka and boots — for further study.

ACKNOWLEDGMENTS

I want to give a heartfelt thank you to everyone at Scholastic, especially Brenda Murray, AnnMarie Anderson, and Kay Petronio. Thank you for a polar adventure.

I also want to thank Jessica Regel and Tara Hart at JVNLA. Thank you for your continued guidance and support.

And I am very grateful to Laura Kissel, polar curator at the Byrd Polar Research Center Archival Program. Thank you for all of your help and for the use of the photos.

SOURCE NOTES

Adams, Mildred. "Dogs that Rank as Heroes Have a Hall of Fame." *New York Times*, January 5, 1930.

American Experience, "Alone on the Ice." Written, produced, and directed by Nancy Porter, 1999. Transcript www.pbs.org/wgbh/amex/ice/filmmore/transcript/transcript1.html.

Bird, William. "Amateurs Helped Byrd Reach Pole." *New York Times*, June 14, 1926.

----. "Byrd in Conference as He Nears Kings Bay." *New York Times*, April 28, 1926.

----. "Byrd Plane Snaps Ski in Second Test." *New York Times*, May 5, 1926.

----. "Byrd Polar Expedition Nearing King's Bay." *New York Times*, April 26, 1926.

Byrd, Richard E. "At the Bottom of the World." *The Youth's Companion*, Vol. 102, Issue 5, May 1928.

----. "At the Bottom of the World." *The Youth's Companion*, Vol. 102, Issue 6, June 1928.

----. "Byrd Begins His Own Story of Polar Flight." *New York Times*, December 2, 1929.

----. "Byrd Extols Spirit of Volunteer Crew." *New York Times*, April 19, 1926.

----. "Byrd Praises Crew in Radio from Ship." *New York Times*, April 11, 1926.

----. "Byrd Starts Own Story of Epic Airplane Flight to North Pole." *Los Angeles Times*, May 14, 1926.

----. "Byrd Tells of Daring Climb in Plane Over Jagged Peaks to Polar Plateau." *New York Times*, December 3, 1929.

----. "Byrd Tells of Scene at South Pole Where He Dropped American Flag." *New York Times*, December 4, 1929.

----. "Byrd Tests Radio on His Way North." *New York Times*, April 22, 1926.

----. "Byrd Writes of Utilizing Winds in Fog." *New York Times*, July 4, 1927.

----. "Byrd's Second Story for the Times." *New York Times*, July 3, 1927.

----. *Exploring with Byrd*. New York: G.P. Putnam's Sons, 1937.

----. "The First Flight to the North Pole." *The Register*, Adelaide, May 18, 1927.

----. *Little America: Aerial Exploration in the Antarctic the Flight to the South Pole*. New York: G.P. Putnam's Sons, 1930.

----. "My Answer to the Challenge of the South." *The Youth's Companion*, Vol. 102, Issue 8, August 1928.

----. "Naval Radio Expert Sailing with Byrd." *New York Times*, April 13, 1926.

----. "New Giant Peaks Are Found by Byrd on Flight South." *New York Times*, November 22, 1929.

----. *Skyward*. New York: Blue Ribbon Books, 1928.

----. "What the North Pole Looks Like!— ." *Los Angeles Times*, June 20, 1926.

Calhoun, C.H. "Admiral Byrd's Terrier Igloo Knows the Two Polar Regions." *New York Times*, June 22, 1930.

Chicago Daily Tribune. "Admiral Byrd at Burial of Igloo, His Pet Terrier." June 1, 1931.

----. "Dog Taken Ill, Admiral Byrd Cancels Tour." April 21, 1931.

Cowan, Francis D. "Byrd Ship Enters Pacific Doldrums." *New York Times*, October 1, 1928.

Czech, Kenneth P. "First to Fly over the North Pole." *Aviation History*, May 1998.

The Deseret News, "Bennett Will Be Buried as One of Nation's Heroes." April 26, 1928.

Fitzhugh, Green. "Dick Byrd — Adventurer." *Popular Science Monthly*, June 1928.

----."Dick Byrd — Adventurer." *Popular Science Monthly*, July 1928.

----. "Dick Byrd — Adventurer." *Popular Science Monthly*, August 1928.

----. "Dick Byrd — Adventurer." *Popular Science Monthly*, September 1928.

Gould, Lawrence M. "Gould Diary Tells of Wait for Rescue." *New York Times*, March 29, 1929.

Kimball, James H. "Telling Ocean Flyers when to Hop." *Popular Science Monthly*, July 1928.

Leep, Mary. "These Dogs Will Brave the Antarctic." *New York Times*, March 11, 1928.

Literary Digest, "Dick Byrd as a Mercury of Modern Flying Science." July 23, 1927.

Los Angeles Times. "Byrd Tells of Arctic Flight." January 20, 1926.

----. "Nation Listens to Byrd Report." June 24, 1930.

Mabie, Janet. "Dogs First — Then Planes." *New McClure's*, Vol. 61, Issue 1, July 1928.

Murphy, Charles J.V. *Struggle: The Life and Exploits of Commander Richard E. Byrd*. New York: Frederick A. Stokes Company, 1928.

New York Times. "$25,000 Orteig Prize Long Standing Offer." April 10, 1927.

----. "Antarctic Dog Lost, Radio Helps in Hunt." September 18, 1930.

----. "Bad Weather at Start of Paris Hop." June 30, 1927.

----. "Bennett Rests Again after Vigil at Radio." July 2, 1927.

----. "Bennett Took Rank Among Best Pilots." April 26, 1928.

----. "Byrd and the America." July 3, 1927.

----. "Byrd Declines Dog Gift." April 23, 1931.

----. "Byrd Expedition to Start Monday." March 30, 1926.

----. "Byrd Names Men Aiding Polar Flight." April 5, 1926.

----. "Byrd on High Seas Headed for Tromso." April 7, 1926.

----. "Byrd's Paris Flight Off Until Tuesday." June 19, 1927.

----. "Byrd Party Leaves on First Leg of Trip to Explore Arctic." April 6, 1926.

----. "Byrd Plane Crashes in Its First Trial." April 17, 1927.

----. "Byrd Planned Trip to Arctic for Years." April 4, 1926.

----. "Byrd Ship Ready to Sail Tomorrow." April 4, 1926.

----. "Byrd to Try Flight to Paris in Spring for $25,000 Prize." February 9, 1927.

----. "Byrd Trip May Be Canceled." April 18, 1927.

----. "Byrd Will Carry a Curtiss Oriole." April 2, 1926.

----. "Capital Hails Byrd in Day of Triumph." June 21, 1930.

----. "Deeds of Daring Mark Byrd's Life." November 30, 1929.

----. "Desperate Air Voyage Added to Byrd's Fame." March 12, 1957.

----. "Dog Handlers Set Meeting for Here." December 25, 1927.

----. "Eight Byrd Men Back; Casual on Hardships." April 26, 1930.

----. "George Tennant, Byrd's Ex-Chef, 70." February 16, 1953.

----. "Hard Work Gave Byrd His Fame." December 8, 1921.

----. "Igloo, Byrd's Dog Buried: The Burial of Igloo, Veteran of Two Polar Conquests." June 1, 1931.

----. "Igloo, Byrd's Dog, Polar Hero, Is Dead: Igloo, with Admiral Byrd." April 22, 1931.

----. "M'Kinley Recounts Filming Pole Trip." April 21, 1930.

----. "Of Flight Weather Byrd's Called Worst." July 2, 1927.

----. "Paris Is Byrd's Goal." June 29, 1927.

----. "Raymond Orteig, Hotel Man, Dies." June 8, 1939.

----. "The America's Flight." July 2, 1927.

Owen, Russell. "Achievements of the Byrd Expedition." *New York Times*, February 23, 1930.

----. "Animal Actors in the Antarctic Drama." February 22, 1931.

----. "Antarctic Trails Wear Out Old 'Spy'." *New York Times*, April 4, 1929.

----. "At the Old Antarctic Home." *New York Times*, August 22, 1930.

----. "Bay Ice Breaks Up at Little America." *New York Times*, December 31, 1929.

----. "Byrd as a Small Boy Circled the World Alone." *New York Times*, July 4, 1926.

----. "Byrd Broadcast Brought Home Near." *New York Times*, April 11, 1929.

----. "Byrd Camp Digs Out." *Los Angeles Times*, September 24, 1929.

----. "Byrd Checking Up on Supplies." *Los Angeles Times*, October 16, 1928.

----. "Byrd Crews Feel Tang of Icy Wind." *New York Times*, December 4, 1928.

----. "Byrd Fliers Survey Rockefeller Range." *New York Times*, March 10, 1929.

----. "Byrd Gives Ailing Dog Bunk in His Own Room." *The Milwaukee Journal*, April 4, 1929.

----. "Byrd Hugs Shelter in Antarctic Gale." *New York Times*, December 21, 1928.

----. "Byrd Maps Dangerous Flight over South Pole." *Los Angeles Times*, August 4, 1929.

----. "Byrd Men 'Dig in' at 47 Below." *New York Times*, April 2, 1929.

----. "Byrd Men Endure Record Cold Spell." *New York Times*, July 19, 1929.

----. "Byrd Leaps into Icy Sea to Rescue One of His Men as Barrier Cliff Caves in." *New York Times*, February 2, 1929.

----. "Byrd Plows Pack Toward His Base." *New York Times*, December 17, 1928.

----. "Byrd Safely Flies to South Pole and Back." *New York Times*, November 30, 1929.

----. "Byrd Sleds Jump Off." *Los Angeles Times*, October 17, 1929.

----. "Byrd's Geological Party Starts 400-Mile Trek to Mountains." *New York Times*, November 5, 1929.

----. "Chinook Vanishes into Antarctica." January 24, 1929.

----. *The Conquest of the North and South Poles: Adventures of the Peary and Byrd Expeditions.* New York: Random House, 1952.

----. "Daring Aerial Feat Saved Byrd's Men." *New York Times*, March 24, 1929.

----. "Dogs that Took the Trail with Byrd." *New York Times*, May 11, 1930.

----. "Eerie Nights Mantle Byrd." *Los Angeles Times*, May 18, 1929.

----. "Fought Vainly All Day to Keep to Keep Plane on Ground." *Milwaukee Journal*, March 21, 1929.

----. "'Good to Be Back,' Byrd Exclaims; Now Turns to South Pole Flight." *New York Times*, July 19, 1922.

----. "Ice Break-Up Rips Byrd's Anchorage." *New York Times*, January 21, 1929.

----. "Iggie Cheers Byrd Crew." *Los Angeles Times,* July 29, 1929.

----. "Lindbergh Has Blazed a New Air Trail." May 29, 1927.

----. *South of the Sun.* New York: The John Day Company, 1934.

----. "Veteran Aviators Flying to the Pole." *New York Times*, November 29, 1929.

Potter, Paul. "Ever Wonder What Byrd Ate at South Pole?" *Chicago Daily Tribune,* February 13, 1931.

Rodgers, Eugene. *Beyond the Barrier: The Story of Byrd's First Expedition to Antarctica.* Annapolis, MD: Naval Institute Press, 1990.

Rose, Lisle A. *Explorer: The Life of Richard E. Byrd,* Columbia, MO: University of Missouri Press, 2008.

Saunders, Hortense. "Home Cooking for Explorers on Expedition on Antarctic." *The Southeast Missourian,* July 9, 1928.

Stern, Daniel. "Supplies Educational Films to Promote Better Workmanship." *American Artisan and Hardware Record,* vol. 78, no.11, September 13, 1919.

The Schulenburg Sticker, "Modern Home Aided Byrd Pole Dash." (Schulenburg, Texas) September 17, 1926.

Sullivan, Paul. "The Admiral's Quarters." *Boston Globe,* February 8, 2007.

The Telegraph Herald. "A Great Educational Work." January 23, 1927.

To the Pole: The Diary and Notebook of Richard E. Byrd 1925–1927, edited by Raimund E. Goerler. Columbus, OH: Ohio State University Press, 1998.

Walden, Jane Brevoort. *Igloo.* New York: G.P. Putnam's Sons, 1931.

Ware, Foster. "Weather Bureau Plays a Large Role in Flying." *New York Times,* June 19, 1927.

Who's Who in the Nation's Capital 1921–22. Washington, DC: The Consolidated Publishing Company, 1921.

Wilson, P.W. "The Attack on the Pole." *Boy's Life,* July 1926.

With Byrd at the South Pole. Dir. Joseph T. Rucker and Willard Van der Veer. Paramount Pictures, 1930.

The Youth's Companion, "A Message From the Bottom of the World." Vol. 103, Issue 6, June 1929.

INDEX

185